SIMONE WEIL

MODERN SPIRITUAL MASTERS
Robert Ellsberg, Series Editor

This series introduces the writing and vision of some of the great spiritual masters of the twentieth century. Along with selections from their writings, each volume includes a comprehensive introduction, presenting the author's life and writings in context, and drawing attention to points of special relevance to contemporary spirituality.

Some of these authors found a wide audience in their lifetimes. In other cases recognition has come long after their deaths. Some are rooted in long-established traditions of spirituality. Others charted new, untested paths. In each case, however, the authors in this series have engaged in a spiritual journey shaped by the influences and concerns of our age. Such concerns include the challenges of modern science, religious pluralism, secularism, and the quest for social justice.

At the dawn of a new millennium this series commends these modern spiritual masters, along with the saints and witnesses of previous centuries, as guides and companions to a new generation of seekers.

Already published:
Dietrich Bonhoeffer (edited by Robert Coles)
Henri Nouwen (edited by Robert A. Jonas)

Forthcoming volumes include:
Pierre Teilhard de Chardin
Karl Rahner
Oscar Romero
John Main
Flannery O'Connor
Brother Roger of Taizé

MODERN SPIRITUAL MASTERS SERIES

SIMONE WEIL

Writings Selected
with an Introduction by

ERIC O. SPRINGSTED

ORBIS BOOKS

Maryknoll, New York 10545

Third printing March 2003

The Catholic Foreign Mission Society of America (Maryknoll) recruits and trains people for overseas missionary service. Through Orbis Books, Maryknoll aims to foster the international dialogue that is essential to mission. The books published, however, reflect the opinions of their authors and are not meant to represent the official position of the society.

Manufactured in the United States of America

Library of Congress Cataloging-in-Publication Data

Weil, Simone, 1909–1943.
    [Selections. English. 1998]
    Simone Weil / writings selected with an introduction by Eric O. Springsted.
        p. cm. – (Modern spiritual masters series)
    ISBN 1-57075-204-4 (pbk.)
    1. Spiritual life. I. Springsted, Eric O. II. Title.
III. Series
B2430.W472E55   1998
194 – dc21

                                     98-19259

In Memory of
Henry Leroy Finch, Jr.
Peter Winch

Contents

Acknowledgments

This book was prepared while I was a resident member at the Center of Theological Inquiry in Princeton, New Jersey, and I wish to thank the Center for its generous support during that time. I also wish to thank Robert Ellsberg of Orbis Books for his initiative in this series and for his invitation to do this work. Acknowledgment is also gratefully extended for the right to publish the essays and translations contained herein:

"Letter to Joë Bousquet" from *Seventy Letters;* "The Love of God and Affliction," "Some Thoughts on the Love of God," "Some Reflections on the Love of God," from *Science, Necessity and the Love of God;* "Draft for a Statement of Human Obligations," from *Selected Essays: 1934– 1943;* selections from *First and Last Notebooks.* All edited and translated by Sir Richard Rees. Reprinted by permission of The Peters Fraser and Dunlop Group Limited on behalf of: © Oxford University Press, 1965, 1968, 1962, 1970.

Selections from *The Notebooks of Simone Weil,* translated by Arthur Wills (London: Routledge & Kegan Paul, 1976); and from *The Need for Roots,* translated by Arthur Wills (London: Routledge & Kegan Paul, 1952). Reprinted by permission of Routledge.

"Reflections on the Right Use of School Studies with a View to the Love of God" translated by Emma Crauford. Reprinted by permission of the Putnam Publishing Group from *Waiting for God,* by Simone Weil. Copyright © 1951, G. P. Putnam's Sons; Renewed © 1979 by G. P. Putnam's Sons.

"Are We Struggling for Justice?" translated by Marina Barabas, *Philosophical Investigations* 10, no. 1 (January 1987). Reprinted by permission of Blackwell Publishers.

"The Prologue" translated by Joan Dargan, © Joan Dargan. Reprinted by permission of the translator.

"Theory of the Sacraments" and selections from *Ecrits de Londres,* translated by Eric O. Springsted, © Eric O. Springsted.

Selections from Simone Weil, *Ecrits de Londres, La Connaissance surnaturelle,* and *Pensées sans ordre concernant l'amour de Dieu,* © Gallimard, 1957, 1950, 1962, translated with permission of Gallimard.

Abbreviations

CS   *La Connaissance surnaturelle*. Paris: Gallimard, 1950.

EL   *Ecrits de Londres*. Paris: Gallimard, 1957.

FLN   *First and Last Notebooks*. Trans. R. Rees. London: Oxford University Press, 1970.

GG   *Gravity and Grace*. Trans. A. Wills. New York: G. P. Putnam's Sons, 1953.

NB   *The Notebooks of Simone Weil*. 2 vols. Trans. A. Wills. London: Routledge & Kegan Paul, 1956.

NR   *The Need for Roots*. Trans. A. Wills. London: Routledge & Kegan Paul, 1952.

SE   *Selected Essays 1934–43*. Trans. R. Rees. London: Oxford University Press, 1962.

SL   *Seventy Letters*. Trans. R. Rees. London: Oxford University Press, 1965.

SN   *On Science, Necessity and the Love of God*. Trans. R. Rees. London: Oxford University Press, 1968.

WG   *Waiting for God*. Trans. E. Crauford. New York: Harper & Row, 1973.

Introduction

The twentieth century has not lacked seriousness. That very seriousness, however, has not always provided very well for either the human spirit or body. Instead, we have been in the midst of a lightning storm of moral, social, and religious clashes. The very things that we need to save us seem the very things that would destroy us. As a result we often wonder if there is any real spiritual bread when having sought it we have gotten only stones and serpents instead; we withdraw then into our own private reveries, threatened by and suspicious of that which ought to draw us together. Yet the century's seriousness has also produced some wonderful examples of genuine inspiration; we have not been without some of history's clearest witnesses to a life of light and grace and to genuine compassion for others.

Simone Weil was one of those witnesses. Possessed of a rare and pure intensity of spirit and an unusual combination of personal commitment and a high and clear intelligence, she has spoken clearly to those who have sought both justice in human affairs and light in matters of the spirit. Yet in a time of clashing moral commitments and spiritual ideals, it is not surprising to find that, less than a beacon in the storm, she has functioned something more like a lightning rod attracting both positive and negative charges, attracting and focusing them. The way she has done so, though, is highly unusual. The reactions to what she did in her life and what she wrote do not fall along a dividing line among already clearly demarcated positions, say between the religious and non-religious, or between liberal and conservative. In thinking on her life and thought, positive and negative come *within* those categories. For she has attracted the deep appreciation of many whose lives are lived outside the Christian church and has attracted some hostility from those within it. T. S. Eliot described her as "at the same time more truly a lover of order and hierarchy than most of those who call themselves Conservative, and more truly a lover of the people than most of those who call themselves Socialist" (NR viii).

The radically different valences assigned to Simone Weil have to many thinkers touched by her bespoken a pure spirit, perhaps one of genius and insight, but one which is also sometimes confused and contradictory. There may be some of that, but, I think, it is much less than would serve to make us comfortable. She herself in the last months of her life seemed to be surprised at how coherent the various traces of her thought really were. Writing to her parents, she claimed that she had discovered something solid and dense, something of pure gold, in her thinking. She worried deeply that it would be obscured because people would look at her, and not at that deposit of gold, somewhat like St. Augustine who complained of those students who when he pointed to the sky would look at his finger instead. If Weil was right, and I am more than inclined to think that she was, then the positive and negative charges that she has attracted may well be reflections of our confusions. That she has acted like a lightning rod may well be because she has put in balance the opposing valences that have made our moral and spiritual seriousness such a storm, and it is we who strike at it to restore our preferred imbalance. Because we are so serious, we assume that it is she who has only half the truth.

That is to put it in such a way that borders nearly on the hagiographic, and Weil would have detested that. Therefore let me say somewhat more specifically and quickly just what it is that is important in her thought and that, because it does run against the grain of much of the century's orthodoxy, both attracts people to her and repels them at the same time. It is, I believe, the sense she has of what the moral self is. How we are accustomed to thinking of ourselves as moral and spiritual beings lies so close to us that it is as nearly unrecognizable to us as water must be to the fish. That is, until we are faced with alternatives. It is at that point that we are often stunned and react sharply, as well we might; our very selves are at stake. Simone Weil's distinctive contribution to religious, social, and moral thought lies, I believe, in her sharp insights into what we take ourselves to be and the confusions and blindnesses and limitations therein. Her contribution also lies in the alternative she offers.

All this can be made clearer if we first take a closer look at her life. For it is there that our attractions and repulsions begin.

Simone Weil was born February 3, 1909. Her older brother, André, was destined to become one of the world's greatest mathematicians of his generation. Her father, Bernard, was a physician, and his profession put the Weil family in solid upper-middle-class comfort and respectability. Selma, her mother, put her own considerable abilities untiringly in the service of the advancement of her children's lives. The family background was Jewish, but as with so many Jewish families of the generation that lived between the time of the Dreyfus affair and the discovery of the Holocaust, it felt free to take little notice of the fact, being as fully assimilated as one could be in French society. Weil herself never felt any particular kinship to her ancestry; indeed, she felt some hostility towards it and is almost never generous when discussing Judaism or the Old Testament, excepting some books such as Genesis, Isaiah, and Job. She certainly felt that it did not define her and reacted sharply whenever it was suggested that it did. Nobody but Simone Weil could tell Simone Weil who she was.

Simone was, I think, no less brilliant than her brother. But her genius was very different. André's intelligence as a mathematician, as with most great mathematicians, manifested itself early and in the most apparent ways. In a family where intelligence was terrifically important, this caused Simone no small amount of anxiety. How that "inferiority" was felt by her, however, is actually an important clue to where her own capacities lay. For she says in a letter that is one of the rare places in all her writings where she talks extensively about herself, that it was not the lack of visible successes that bothered her, "but what did grieve me was the idea of being excluded from that transcendent kingdom to which only the truly great have access and wherein truth

abides" (WG 64). What brought her out of what appears to be
a serious adolescent crisis of identity was the thought that that
kingdom was accessible not only by pure intelligence but could
be entered also if one desires truth and concentrates one's whole
being on it. Under the name of truth she adds, "I also included
beauty, virtue, and every kind of goodness, so that for me it was
a question of the relationship between grace and desire. The con-
viction that had come to me was that when one hungers for bread
one does not receive stones" (WG 64). That idea of moral concentration, the idea of "attention," is central to her genius. For
her it is what distinguishes the truly great from the merely tal-
ented; throughout her writings she applies it severely. Although at
this point such a notion held no religious connotations for her —
she said she saw the problem of God as insoluble and therefore
left it alone — it would bloom in her religious thought.

To say, however, that she had no visible intellectual successes
would be wrong. She was educated in the elite schools of the best
French intellectual tradition. She studied at the Lycée Henri IV
under the philosopher Alain, who gave her his deepest respect
and, in his own emphasis on human action, the earliest shape to
her own thinking. She was one of the first women to graduate
from the prestigious École Normale Supérieure, with the degree
of *agregée de philosophie,* which was reserved for the top few
graduates. But even there and in subsequent teaching positions
in the French *lycée* system, to which her degree gave her access,
it was her moral commitment that is remembered. Her moral
intensity and active involvement in leftist causes earned her the
nicknames of "The Red Virgin" and "The Categorical Imperative
in Skirts." Simone de Beauvoir describes her one meeting with
Weil during their university days. Beauvoir recounts that already
at that time Weil had established a somewhat intimidating repu-
tation. Coming upon Weil in a courtyard of the Sorbonne while
Weil was holding forth on the need for revolution in order to feed
the masses, Beauvoir recalls that her own offering to the conversation was the philosopher's opinion that what the people really
needed was meaning in their lives. Weil frostily replied, quickly
looking her over, that it was clear that she had not ever gone

hungry, a remark that Beauvoir recognized as putting her and her philosophy in its place as belonging to the petty bourgeoisie. (Yet, Beauvoir adds, what was most impressive to her about Weil was not the intimidating moral severity; it was the story recounted of how when Weil read of an earthquake in China she had wept openly at the thought of the destruction. Here was a heart that beat across the world.) Weil was no more accommodating to those in authority such as the director of the École and her thesis advisor, Leon Brunschvig, the great Pascal scholar, constantly posing challenges to their authority.

That sort of personality, of course, has consequences. She never did get along with Brunschvig, and he did not appreciate much her diploma thesis on Descartes. It is perhaps because of this mutual antipathy that Weil never saw much in Pascal, although philosophically they seem to have much in common. When it came time to assign her to a teaching position, the authorities deliberately put her in small provincial towns away from the great centers of the workers' movements in which she was so deeply involved. But even there she could not be kept quiet. Living as thriftily as possible, she donated the additional pay to which her *agregée* entitled her to workers' movements. When not in class, she taught night classes to workers and associated freely with them, something that scandalized the bourgeois parents of her students, whose educational ambitions for their children were clearly more aimed at social advancement than the "kingdom of truth." They were further scandalized when in the town of Le Puy she even managed to lead a strike of the unemployed, a feat whose paradoxicalness seems not to have fazed her in the least.

These are simply anecdotes, enlightening as they might be. Far more important to understanding her is the year she spent working in three factories in Paris in 1934–35. Weil had recently written an essay titled "Reflections concerning the Causes of Liberty and Social Oppression." It was a masterful, yet sympathetic critique of Marx and an attempt to understand how dignity could be found in human labor. Marx had given an analysis of the relations between human thought and dignity and the larger economic enterprise, she argued, that was truly formidable. Rather

than individual thought shaping and controlling such an enterprise, he recognized that it was the other way around. Thought
came out of and was conditioned by the "material conditions
of existence." In this sense, human thought was not free, and
human beings were cogs in the larger economic enterprise. This
insight Weil extended to modern technology, arguing that it was
no longer capitalists that ran the economy, but technocrats. But
even they were not really in charge. They, too, were simply part
of the larger whole, a point that is hardly exhausted sixty years
later.

But therein is a problem. If we are so determined by the material conditions of existence, how then could there be human
dignity? How could humans have some charge of their destiny?
Marx, she thought, gave no satisfactory solution; his analysis was
so good it seemed that his own solutions ran contrary to what
he had already established. Where there were possibilities, Weil
contended, was in the recognition that human labor was always
subject to necessity. If we cannot escape necessity, human dignity
can nevertheless be achieved if the human mind can come to recognize this necessity and can freely give itself to it, making the
necessity its own, something not simply external. Practically this
meant structuring labor so that workers could get some sense of
the larger project, both within the factory and in the larger social
whole. The project could then be morally theirs. The essay is insightful and particularly mature. But it was typical of Weil that
she was not entirely satisfied with it. As a result, faithful to what
Alain had taught her, she therefore sought to revise her thinking
by actually coming into contact with the object of thought. Thus
she entered the factories, to feel in her own being the structures
that others only talked about.

Her experience was not that of a spectator. Despite the family
cushion readily available to her (which her mother was ever ready
to provide — sometimes even without Simone being aware of it),
she lived in a small flat in a working-class section of Paris and
only on the wages she had earned. She fully expected that this
project would not be easy; she was not after all very sanguine
about the conditions workers were subjected to in the depres-

sion of the 1930s. It does seem, though, that she initially believed that she would discover something of human dignity in a sort of workers' stoicism and camaraderie. The expectation was brutally destroyed. There is certainly a sense in which the experience was harder on her than it would be for most people. Weil was maladroit and had a hard time keeping up with the piece work rate that was commonplace in factories of the time. Physically it wreaked havoc on her health, which, since she also suffered from severe migraines, was not strong. More important, she came to recognize that labor in those conditions was universally humiliating, that it destroyed all sense of human dignity. She recognized that in the factory system the worker counted for nothing. Given her earlier analysis, that was not entirely surprising. What was surprising was the discovery that in the course of time the worker came to count for nothing in his or her own eyes or anybody else's for that matter. The humiliation went to the depths of the soul. So Weil discovered "affliction" (*malheur*), a condition to which one could not consent, a condition that in its very nature could never be ennobling. Affliction had the literal ability to kill the soul and everything that makes us human, even though the body continued on. This included any sense of rights, of initiative, of expectation of respect from others, of hope itself. This discovery shattered all her earlier optimism.

Weil, of course, was able to leave the factory and did so at the end of August 1935. Brutalizing as the experience had been, it did not keep her from further attempts to learn by actual contact. She could never be content with watching from afar. Interspersed with teaching and sick leaves over the next three years, she also worked on a farm and, although a pacifist at the time, joined the anarchist-syndicalist elements in the Spanish Civil War. Again, she found even good causes tainted; she learned not only of fascist butchery but that of her own comrades who executed a priest and a fifteen-year-old boy who refused to join them. A clumsy accident — she stepped into a pot of cooking oil — soon forced her back home, and probably saved her life, for shortly afterwards the militiamen with whom she served were decimated in battle. In a letter to Georges Bernanos, who also had written of the Spanish

Civil War, she noted the results of her experience: "one sets out as a volunteer, with the idea of sacrifice, and finds oneself in a war which resembles a war of mercenaries, only with much more cruelty and with less human respect for the enemy"(SL 109).

It was in the midst of these unsettling years that Weil's life took a profound spiritual turn. That turn, and this is particularly important to understanding her, is not away from what she had already learned. It took place within it.

In the letter known as her "spiritual autobiography" Weil describes three "contacts" with Christianity that "really counted." The first took place shortly after the factory experience. Taken by her parents to Portugal to recover, she recounts that one night while alone in a small, "wretched" fishing village she watched a procession take place among the villagers in honor of their patron saint. She, too, felt wretched, the discovery of affliction having burned itself into her, like the brand on the head of a slave.

> It was evening and there was a full moon over the sea. The wives of the fishermen were, in procession, making a tour of all the ships, carrying candles and singing what must certainly be very ancient hymns of heartrending sadness. Nothing can give any idea of it.... There the conviction was suddenly borne in upon me that Christianity is preeminently the religion of slaves, that slaves cannot help belonging to it, and I among others. (WG 67)

The second she more briefly describes when she tells of how in 1937 while at Assisi, "I was compelled for the first time in my life to go down on my knees." The third is more extensive, and the account is deeply related to the way that she would subsequently articulate Christian spirituality.

In 1938, Weil and her mother attended Holy Week services at Solesmes, a monastery known for a distinctive form of chant. At the outset, the intention seems to have been primarily aesthetic. In the course of the week, she met a "young English Catholic" (although it may have been actually an American Rhodes Scholar, Charles Bell) who introduced her to the English metaphysical poets, especially George Herbert. She quickly memorized Herbert's poem "Love" and recited it to herself regularly, particularly in the midst of a headache. "It was during one of these recitations that . . . Christ himself came down and took possession of me" (WG 69).

When dealing with Simone Weil, there is too often a tendency to peek at her life behind what she says, as if she were simply writing in code of her own life. She rarely is. What she says of this experience, however, is vitally important to understanding the nature of her spiritual writings in at least two ways. First, it says something about the nature of faith and the supernatural in Weil's thinking. She makes it quite clear that she did not reason herself into faith. Indeed, she says that afterwards "I still half refused, not my love but my intelligence" (WG 69). But she was no less certain for that. For what she felt in the midst of her suffering was "the presence of a love, like that which one can read in the smile on a beloved face." Faith was not an intellectual position for her, although it clearly had profound intellectual consequences. It responded to something that intellect had only glimmers of and that shapes in time how we use our intellect. It was a capacity given by grace, given by God's own possession, to read goodness and love, and to respond to it, just as we read the smile on a beloved face.

Second, affliction now appeared in a much different light. She suddenly recognized that love and goodness did not have to be defeated even by affliction, that even in the midst of soul-destroying suffering God could be present. Indeed, as she came to outline in "The Love of God and Affliction," in affliction God could be *perfectly* present, just as he was to the afflicted Christ on the Cross. If the discovery of affliction marked the end of a belief that humans by understanding the structure of necessity could consent to it and be ennobled, in the experience of Christ, Weil's thinking about affliction was given a new cast. It could be a way of giving one's total consent to God, who never refuses his love to those who wait for it. Affliction could serve to erase the screen of the self that we erect between us and God and cannot tear down by ourselves. She notes: "The supernatural greatness of Christianity lies in the fact that it does not seek a supernatural remedy for suffering but a supernatural use for it" (GG 132).

The Solesmes experience marks a clear transformation in Weil's thinking. From then on she begins to produce, in addition to her social and political works, a vast corpus of spiritual and philosophical writings whose Christian emphasis is explicit. But in many ways it is also at that point that Weil's own thinking and person become more recalcitrant to easy discussion. The conversion takes place at a time that she is already beginning to withdraw from much direct and organized political involvement. At the same time, her attempts at putting herself in contact with the world actually intensify, but often in a way that puzzles us.

When Hitler invaded Prague, Weil gave up the pacifism that she held with so many intellectuals of the decade. Soon after that, disappointed that Paris was not defended, she was forced to flee quite reluctantly with her parents to Marseilles when the Nazis marched into the capital. It was in Marseilles that a whole series of new projects came to occupy her. She, like others, did what she could to undermine the Nazi effort, distributing anti-Nazi literature and visiting the prison camps. She managed to get herself arrested, and quite typically gave no ground to the judge. It was also during this period that she again spent time working on a farm, that of the philosopher Gustave Thibon. And again, she eschewed any comfort, choosing not to live with the family but in an old hut.

But most important was a plan that she began to develop at this point for a corps of front-line nurses. Apparently inspired by old Germanic sagas which told of young maidens who at the front of battle inspired the troops and gave them a visible reminder of the land and people for which they were fighting, Weil hoped to establish a corps of young women who would be parachuted into the front lines to care for the wounded in the midst of battle. Because it was so dangerous (death was nearly inevitable), but so freely done and solely for reasons of compassion, she believed that it would serve as a witness to what the Allies were fighting for. War, she knew, even when entered into for the best of motives, soon came to possess men's souls, making them blind. Such an action she hoped would tip the balance back again. Of course, she meant to be one of those who put herself in harm's way.

It was in hope of putting this plan into action that Weil allowed herself to join her parents in leaving Marseilles for New York, for she hoped that from there she could get back to the war zone in France. After a brief period in New York, she managed through contacts with the Free French in London to get as far as London. There she was set to work on writing a number of analyses and reports that would address the problems that needed to be dealt with when a legitimate government was returned to France after the war. Her output was tremendous, including the book *The Need for Roots,* and involves a truly distinctive and new approach to political and social problems. Crucial to this approach were two elements. First was her insistence that social life be oriented around the moral category of obligations rather than rights, as it had been since the French revolution. Second was the idea that social life be rooted, rooted both in a past, but just as vitally, through labor, in the natural world of necessity itself. Her thought had come full circle, returning to the same issues that had occupied her at the beginning of her career. They were, however, now transformed in the light of faith. Yet, it was still action that preoccupied her, and all this work meant little to her without the nurses project.

But the project was not to be. De Gaulle thought it mad. Weil herself collapsed in the spring of 1943, suffering from tuberculosis, exacerbated by overwork. The prognosis for recovery was not dim, but in an era without penicillin and when tuberculosis was treated by rest and overeating, Weil proved an intractable patient. A person who had always seen in food something belonging to the moral order and who therefore had regularly and consciously eaten slightly, she simply refused to eat more than she thought people in occupied France were getting. (This was a fast, if we may use that word, she had begun before her collapse, although in all likelihood she knew before arriving in London that she had tuberculosis.) As a result her condition worsened, and she died on August 23, 1943, at Ashford, Kent.

Here we begin to see a sort of eccentricity — a life lived outside

the center to which we are accustomed — that does attract and
repel at the same time. It is underlined by her personal religious
life after her conversion. On the one hand, it is highly attractive, beautiful in its attention and clarity. We see this not only
in her writings, but in her practices. While working on Gustave
Thibon's farm she says that she developed the practice of reciting
the Lord's Prayer each morning in Greek, with "absolute attention." The effect, she says, was extraordinary: "The infinity of
the ordinary expanses of perception is replaced by an infinity to
the second or sometimes the third degree. At the same time, fill-
ing every part of this infinity of infinity, there is silence, a silence
which is not the absence of sound but which is the object of a
positive sensation, more positive than that of sound." Moreover,
she adds: "Sometimes during this recitation or at other moments,
Christ is really present with me in person" (WG 72). In New
York she regularly attended not only Mass but black churches
in Harlem, finding both the people, the ones not in power, and
their freedom quite to her taste. Yet, on the other hand, her faith
was anything but exultant. She steadfastly refused baptism until
on her death bed when it was performed by an unordained friend.
But even then she never actually participated in the Eucharist that
she had so steadfastly contemplated in Catholic churches. Her
"spiritual autobiography" is actually written to explain why she
could not enter the church.

The "spiritual autobiography" is one of a series of letters that
Weil wrote to Father J. M. Perrin, a blind Dominican priest who
became her close friend and confidant in Marseilles. He was
greatly impressed by her incredible understanding of the univer-
sality of grace, and it was under his pressing that she wrote the
series of essays on the ancient Greeks that is so central to her
thought. As she explains it to him, she is particularly fearful of
the "social nature" of the church, a sort of group think that all
too often substitutes for genuine focus on God. More exactly, she
feels so attracted to it that it is a temptation she feels she has to
resist, for to join the church would alter her. She gives a number
of reasons for not becoming a Catholic, including a sense that
she would betray those outside the church. These included not

only the ancient Greeks, but those from numerous other spiritual traditions from which she had gained so much. Her writing and insights, Christian as they may be, owe much to her reading of these sources, including many Eastern ones such as the *Bhagavad Gîta* and the *Upanishads*. She was not about to give them up, and the church's refusal to accept such outsiders smacked of totalitarianism. But the crucial reason as she tells it is the feeling that God did not want her in the church. And for her, obedience to God was the heart of the matter. She notes that even if her salvation were lying on the table, she would not pick it up unless commanded.

It is at this point that the unsettling parts of Weil's person come through most clearly. There is at once a sort of pride, an immense desire to be great, combined with great diffidence, and, indeed, a certain sort of brutality towards the self. When thinking of Christ's affliction on the Cross, she admits to "the sin of envy." (But she knows it is a sin.) She refuses to do anything for herself. And for many of her readers this makes her more of a danger than a guide to be trusted. Her insistence in her writings that our selves need to be "de-created" in order to fully love God and neighbor seems not only perilous, but even, according to some, Manichaean and inhuman.

What are we to make of this? There may well be a sense in which Weil may have been unhealthy, and in which her own experiments in life were less than sensible. Dwelling on that, however, can be terrifically shallow and miss her real importance. Weil never recommended herself as a paradigm for others. Her refusal to join the church was not the result of an argument; it was a vocation to which she felt called and which she could not betray. In her writings she almost never uses "I" for the "I" has no place in spirituality. But that is a clue to where she is helpful. If she was sometimes less than careful about her own person, she was interested in truth and she was fully convinced that truth is not an abstraction but something that exists only in life itself. If "the problem of God" could not be solved by cool, distanced speculation, it could bear fruit, she discovered, by committing one's self to God. Just as the truth about the factory could be gained only by contact, so the truth of life and God can be gained only by contact. And contact comes only when one does not keep herself at a safe distance, surveying the possibilities and deciding ahead of time whether they will be good for us or not. We have to be willing to be transformed by the truth of what we encounter; we cannot seek to control it to our own ends. She may well have recognized the importance of this truth simply because she struggled with it to the degree that she did.

That is why Weil becomes a lightning rod attracting all the charges attaching to our notion of the human self. Her concern is about the truth of human life; we would rather see it differently. The modern sense of the self is constituted by the notion of rights and personal development. Morally, we thus often see ourselves in terms of what we should expect from others and of what we can and ought to do for ourselves. That, at its worst, puts us awash in idolatrous religions of self-affirmation. Those are obvious and shallow. But even at our most refined our sense of human justice tends to be controlled by a metaphor of power development that leads us to believe that by increasing power and sharing it around we will find the human good, a sort of capitalist economy designed for the moral and spiritual self. Just as we think we can help the poor by increasing the economy through additional material production and competition, by increasing wealth, so, too, we often believe that everyone can be morally prosperous by increasing the personal power of individuals. The empowered self is the one that has freedom and autonomy. And that is what it means to us to be fully human. That metaphor is not one of narrow selfishness, for justice is achieved when there is universal empowerment and self-determination. When Weil refuses to use her powers and talents to maintain freedom and autonomy, when she refuses to develop them, it is clear why we begin to regard her as self-destructive. Her death seems a waste, not only of herself to herself, but of somebody who had so much to offer to the moral economy had she lived longer.

Why she thought differently, though, can be understood if we consider what the discovery of affliction revealed to her. Affliction was not simply a problem with a system, although the factory system of her time and many of the systems of the century are particularly effective at producing affliction. It was a universal possibility for the human soul. The human soul *is* fragile and can be destroyed. Oppression — the stifling of empowerment — and unfairness can leave us intact and noble; the problem in those cases is, as Weil thought in her earlier work, a matter of reforming the system. But affliction can seize the soul and undo it. How? As she makes clear in "The Love of God and Affliction," affliction, while including physical suffering, is chiefly a matter of social humiliation, a ceasing to count in anyone's eyes, including one's own. At that point, giving power to the powerless is not possible; there is nobody left inside to wield effective human power in the human world. Power simply burns itself into the soul, making the soul more and more an object of other people's actions, no longer the subject of one's own. Our self is a self that acts among others and requires that they respect our actions; the afflicted, however, no longer direct their own actions. There is nothing to them that can focus human power into a coherent project. They are not effective nor do they affect us any longer. And since affliction has also an essential *accidental* quality to it (*malheur* is literally "bad fortune"), one who is afflicted can find no reason for this being so. The mind cannot understand and thus cannot find any way to accept this condition. The world then seems chaotic, purposeless, and poisonous. Hope disappears, and the afflicted inevitably begin to hate themselves. Thus even well-meaning "empowerment" simply makes matters worse. The afflicted become tools of our pity and our own self-image, our exercises of our own moral empowerment, and they recognize it.

The possibility of affliction and the impossibility of "empowerment" as a way of saving the soul from destruction thus signaled for Weil not only a practical problem with modern understandings of the person and of justice; they also signaled that the sense of well-being and goodness we derive from empowerment is conceptually *other* than that of perfect goodness. It is an ersatz kingdom. As she puts it, the necessary and the good are different things. We cannot produce goodness by necessity. In her notebooks she claims that if it were not for affliction, we might believe ourselves in paradise. That she thought was a horrid possibility, for it was the possibility that we would continue to live for a goodness that was no more than the projection of the relief of our anxieties. But where is the alternative? Where is perfect love and justice?

It is God's own love in the Cross of Christ. In "The Love of God and Affliction" Weil insists that we see the crucified Christ not as a martyr for truth, or even the king of glory executed out of jealous resentment. For her, Christ is purely and simply afflicted. But Christ does not let his condition change his love for the Father and the world he has created, even though it contains affliction. Even though abandoned, he accepts this as the Father's will and loves even when there seems nothing to love. He is not filled with resentment. And in that, Weil suggests, is ultimately established a bond of perfect love between the abandoned Christ and the Father in heaven, between emptiness and fullness. In Christ's love, God's love is present in the world. That at least means that affliction is not an ultimate evil. But Christ is not simply an example of how we might get through suffering. By accepting emptiness he redeems affliction; by accepting the nothingness of our condition he gives life to a world. Indeed, now necessity is not seen as something hostile, but is, in Plato's words, "persuaded by goodness." His self-emptying is for life, not his own, but the lives of others. When love triumphs over power, and selflessness over autonomy, it is Christ's love in us that is our soul.

If there is a single key to understanding Weil it is that Christ's crucifixion provides the paradigm of perfect love and justice and the means by which human life can be lived at all levels within God's life. In the case of affliction when the self created by the push and pull of necessity is fully de-created, it can make of that state an opportunity for perfect love. God's love can be fully present when there is nothing that stands between God and the human. Weil, moreover, applies the paradigm to creation: in creating a world, God does not create by power; God renounces being all in order that a world might exist.

But it is also crucial to understand that Christ's self-emptying and self-giving love dwells at several levels that encompass life from the fullness of joy to the emptiness of affliction. We do not love God only when we are fully de-created. Thus she insists that there are "implicit forms of the love of God."

> Since the commandment "Thou shalt love the Lord thy God" is laid upon us so imperatively, it is to be inferred that the love in question is not only the love a soul can give or refuse when God comes in person to take the hand of his future bride, but also a love preceding this visit, for a permanent obligation is implied.
>
> This previous love cannot have God for its object, since God is not present to the soul and has never yet been so. It must then have another object. Yet it is destined to become the love of God. We can call it the indirect or implicit love of God. (WG 137)

The implicit loves of God — love of neighbor, love of the beauty of the world, love of religious ceremonies and friendship — have the secret presence of God in them. What makes each a love of God is that in each case human action is constituted not by self-seeking or preservation, but is a matter of opening itself up to the reality of strangers, friends, the natural world, and God's mediated presence in the sacraments. For example, God's love becomes incarnate in us when we pay "attention" to others, putting aside our own interests and projections and letting them reveal themselves to us. That is the sole way of giving life back to the afflicted, for we in giving up our autonomy let them have life again. In waiting on them, we create room for them to act, a space that does not exist when human relations are those of power, even benign power. Additionally, the beauty of the world is revealed to us when technology is replaced by a science that pays attention to the order of the world governed by goodness, a science not dedicated to power, but to the contemplation of the beauty of the world. These implicit loves, Weil says, constitute a preparatory period for the soul and have the virtue of a sacrament. When God is fully present to the soul, they do not disappear; "they become infinitely stronger and all loves taken together make only a single love" (WG 138).

The paradigm even carries through to Weil's later political thought. Replacing the concept of "rights" as the chief political category of justice with that of obligations — the duties we owe others — she seeks to make political justice a matter not of rationally balancing concentrations of power, whether personal or institutional, but of balancing them by direct human interaction. That interaction is a matter of seeking the consent of others, and never violating it. When she calls this sort of justice "impersonal," it is not because it is abstract, but because of what we take the "personal" normally to be. We therefore need to act "impersonally" in order to take persons seriously. And she means us to take individual humans very seriously indeed.

In Colossians 3:10–11, St. Paul talks about "stripping off the old self" and "clothing yourselves with the new self, which is being renewed in knowledge according to the image of its creator." The new self, the self "hid in Christ in God," is the ultimate result of that stripping off of the old self. Similarly "de-creation" in Weil is not self-destruction; it is the putting off an old self in order to be open to becoming a new one. It is finding a new center of human action. In this she has certain parallels to other spiritual masters of the twentieth century such as Thomas Merton, although she is far less gentle with the old self. There have been few of any time who better understood than Weil our self-deceptions and attempts to call the old "new" with little substantial change. Her own dealings with the temptations of self-deception may well have been at the root of that sort of great worry. But in Weil, like Paul and others, what is important and central is that the new self be in the image of its creator. For Weil that image is the image of the Christ who gave up his power to give life to others.

•

The *œuvres complets* of Simone Weil currently being published will be fifteen volumes, an amazing output from one who died so young. Obviously only a small part of that work is reproduced here. Thus the principles of selection should be made apparent to the reader. All selections are taken from the last years of Weil's life, and all essays are from the time she spent in Marseilles on. While these selections can be read in any order (they are not chronological), they are arranged in such a way that as they raise important issues in Weil's thought they will be able to build on what has gone before. Read in order they should be helpful to the reader to seeing the direction of Weil's thinking — from where it conceptually begins to its application. Thus we begin with part 1 on "The Love of God." If there is a single core to Weil's spiritual thought it is the essay "The Love of God and Affliction." The shorter essays and the letter to Joë Bousquet which surround it expand on the insights of that essay. The selection of passages from Weil's notebooks in part 1 are designed to provide briefly some additional sense of important distinctions that arise in the essays, conceptions such as that of "necessity" and its relation to "goodness." Part 2 highlights some of Weil's most important reflections on the nature of religion. The notebook selections here are grouped to raise certain conceptual contributions that Weil has to make about how we discuss the nature of the supernatural, mystery, and the nature of faith. As we noted above, Weil never deserted her concern for problems of social life and justice. In part 3 we have included one of the most important essays for understanding her sense of justice, as well as the "credo" she wanted to propose for leaders of a just society. The selections at the beginning raise crucial concepts regarding the nature of human cultural associations and can help give some sense of the context in which she thought justice needs to be instantiated. It is also hoped that the combination of full essays and notebook selections will give the reader some sense of the full range of *how* Weil wrote and thought, for her style, which rarely uses the word "I," underlines the nature of the thought that it expresses.

Prologue

There are two copies of this text, one of which is headed by the note: "Beginning of the book (the book which should contain these thoughts and many others)." The other has the title "Prologue." There is much debate as to whether this records an actual experience of Weil. Its content shows important similarities to Herbert's poem "Love."

He entered my room and said: "You miserable creature, you who understand nothing and know nothing. Come with me and I'll teach you of things you cannot even imagine." I followed him.

He led me into a church. It was new and ugly. He brought me before the altar and said, "Kneel down." I said to him, "I haven't been baptized." He told me, "Fall down on your knees before this place with love, as before the place where truth is to be found." I obeyed.

He made me go out and then climb up to an attic with an open window from which one could see the whole city, wooden scaffolding, the river where boats were being unloaded. Inside the attic were only a table and two chairs. He made me sit down.

We were alone. He spoke. Once in a while someone would come in, join in the conversation, and then leave.

It was no longer winter. It wasn't yet springtime. The tree branches were bare, without buds, out in the cold and sun.

Daylight would climb, dazzle, and fade, and then moon- and starlight would come in through the window. Then once again the morning sun would arise.

Occasionally he would grow silent and take a loaf of bread

from the shelf, and we would share it. That bread truly had the taste of bread. I have never found that taste since.

He would pour out for both of us wine that tasted of the sun and earth where the city had been built.

Sometimes we would stretch out on the attic floor, and the sweetness of sleep would come over me. Then I would wake up again and drink in the sunlight.

He had promised me a teaching, but he didn't teach me at all. We talked about all kinds of things, in no particular fashion, like old friends.

One day he told me, "Go away now." I fell to my knees, I flung my arms around his legs, I begged him not to chase me away. But he threw me out onto the stairs. I went downstairs stunned, my heart shattered. I walked around in the streets. Then I realized I had no idea where that house was.

I have never tried to find it again. I understood that he had only come to get me by mistake. My place is not in that attic. It is anywhere at all, in a prison cell, in one of those bourgeois parlors full of red plush and bibelots, in the waiting room of a train station, anywhere at all — but not in that attic.

I can't keep myself from repeating sometimes, with fear and trembling, some of what he told me. How can I be sure of remembering exactly? He isn't here to tell me.

I know quite well that he doesn't love me. How could he love me? And yet something deep within, a particle of myself, can't help thinking, all the while trembling with fear, that perhaps, in spite of everything, he does love me. (CS 9–10)

1

The Love of God

Love bade me welcome; yet my soul drew back,
Guiltie of dust and sinne.
But quick-ey'd Love, observing me grow slack
From my first entrance in,
Drew nearer to me, sweetly questioning,
If I lacked any thing.

A guest, I answer'd, worthy to be here:
Love said, You shall be he.
I, the unkinde, ungratefull? Ah my deare,
I cannot look on thee.
Love took my hand, and smiling did reply,
Who made the eyes but I?

Truth Lord, but I have marr'd them: let my shame
Go where it doth deserve.
And know you not, sayes Love, who bore the blame?
My deare, then I will serve.
You must sit down sayes Love, and taste my meat:
So I did sit and eat.

(George Herbert, "Love")

LETTER TO JOË BOUSQUET

*Joë Bousquet was a quadriplegic whose spine had been shat-
tered in World War I. Living bedridden in Dourgne, he was
introduced to Weil in 1942. She felt a great deal of friendship*

for him, which comes through in this letter. It also gives one of
the rare instances where she talks about her own experience.

[Marseille] May 12, 1942

Cher Ami,

First of all, thank you for what you have just done for me. If your letter is effective, as I hope, you will have done it, not for me but for others through me, for your younger brothers who should be infinitely dear to you since the same fate has struck them. Perhaps some of them will owe to you, just before the moment of death, the solace of an exchange of sympathy.

You are specially privileged in that the present state of the world is a reality for you. Perhaps even more so than for those who at this moment are killing and dying, wounding and being wounded, because they are taken unawares, without knowing where they are or what is happening to them; and, like you in your time, they are unable to think thoughts appropriate to their situation. As for the others, the people here for example, what is happening is a confused nightmare for some of them, though very few, and for the majority it is a vague background like a theatrical drop-scene. In either case it is unreal.

But you, on the other hand, for twenty years you have been repeating in thought that destiny which seized and then released so many men, but which seized you permanently; and which now returns again to seize millions of men. You, I repeat, are now really equipped to think it. Or if you are still not quite ready — as I think you are not — you have at least only a thin shell to break before emerging from the darkness inside the egg into the light of truth. It is a very ancient image. The egg is this world we see. The bird in it is Love, the Love which is God himself and which lives in the depths of every man, though at first as an invisible seed. When the shell is broken and the being is released, it still has this same world before it. But it is no longer inside. Space is opened and torn apart. The spirit, leaving the miserable body in some corner, is transported to a point outside space, which is not a point of view, which has no perspective, but from which this world is seen as it is, unconfused by perspective. Compared to what it is inside the egg, space has become an infinity to the second or rather the third power. The moment stands still. The whole of space is filled, even though sounds can be heard, with a dense silence which is not an absence of sound but is a positive object of sensation; it is the secret word, the word of Love who holds us in his arms from the beginning.

You, when once you have emerged from the shell, will know the reality of war, which is the most precious reality to know because war is unreality itself. To know the reality of war is the Pythagorean harmony, the unity of opposites; it is the plenitude of knowledge of the real. That is why you are infinitely privileged, because you have war permanently lodged in your body, waiting for years in patient fidelity until you are ripe to know it. Those who fell beside you did not have time to collect their thought from its frivolous wandering and focus it upon their destiny. And those who came back unwounded have all killed their past by oblivion, even if they have seemed to remember it, because war is affliction and it is as easy to direct one's thought voluntarily towards affliction as it would be to persuade an untrained dog to walk into a fire and let itself be burnt. To think affliction, it is necessary to bear it in one's flesh, driven very far in like a nail, and for a long time, so that thought may have time to grow strong enough to regard it. To regard it from outside, having succeeded in leaving the body and even, in a sense, the soul as well. Body and soul remain not only pierced through but nailed down at a fixed point. Whether or not affliction imposes literal immobility, there is always enforced immobility in this sense that a part of the soul is always steeped, monotonously, incessantly, and inextricably, in pain. Thanks to this immobility the infinitesimal seed of divine love placed in the soul can slowly grow and bear fruit in patience — ἐν ὑπομενῇ is the divinely beautiful Gospel expression. Translators say *in patientia,* but ὑπομένειν is quite another thing. It means to remain where one is, motionless, in expectation, unshaken and unmoved by any external shock.

Fortunate are those in whom the affliction which enters their flesh is the same one that afflicts the world itself in their time. They have the opportunity and the function of knowing the truth of the world's affliction and contemplating its reality. And that is the redemptive function itself. Twenty centuries ago, in the Roman Empire, slavery was the affliction of the age, and crucifixion was its extreme expression.

But alas for those who have this function and do not fulfill it.

When you say that you do not feel the difference between good and evil, your words are not serious if taken literally because you are speaking of another man in you who is clearly the evil in you; you are well aware — or when there is any doubt a careful scrutiny can nearly always dispel it — which of your thoughts, words, and deeds strengthen that other man in you at your expense and which ones strengthen you at his. What you mean is that you have not yet consented to recognize this difference as the distinction between good and evil.

It is not an easy consent to give, because it commits one irrevocably. There is a kind of virginity in the soul as regards good, which is lost forever once the soul has given this consent — just as a woman's virginity is lost after she has yielded to a man. The woman may become unfaithful, adulterous, but she will never again be a virgin. So she is frightened when she is about to yield. Love triumphs over this fear.

For every human being there is a point in time, a limit, unknown to anyone and above all to himself, but absolutely fixed, beyond which the soul cannot keep this virginity. If, before this precise moment, fixed from all eternity, it has not consented to be possessed by the good, it will immediately afterwards be possessed in spite of itself by the bad.

A man may yield to the bad at any moment of his life, because he yields to it unconsciously and unaware that he is admitting an external authority into his soul; and before surrendering her virginity to it the soul drugs herself with an opiate. To be possessed by the bad, it is not necessary to have consented to it; but the good never possesses the soul until she has said yes. And such is the fear of consummating the union that no soul has the power to say yes to the good unless she is urgently constrained by the almost immediate approach of the time-limit which will decide her eternal fate. For one man this time-limit may occur at the age of five, for another at the age of sixty. In any case, neither before nor after it has been reached is it possible to locate it temporally; in the sphere of duration this instantaneous and eternal choice can only be seen refracted. For those who have yielded to the bad a long time before the limiting moment is reached, this moment is no longer real. The most a human being can do is to guard intact his faculty for saying yes to the good, until the time when the limiting moment has almost been reached.

It appears to me certain that for you the limiting moment has not yet arrived. I lack the power to read men's hearts, but it seems to me that there are signs that it is not far distant. Your faculty for consent is certainly intact.

I think that when you have consented to the good you will break the shell, after an interval perhaps, but doubtless a short one; and the moment you are outside it there will be pardon for that bullet which once pierced the center of your body, and thus also for the whole universe which drove it there.

The intelligence has a part in preparing the nuptial consent to God. It consists in looking at the evil in oneself and hating it. Not trying to get rid of it, but simply descrying it and keeping one's eyes fixed upon it until one feels repulsion — even before one has said yes to its opposite.

I believe that the root of evil, in everybody perhaps, but certainly in those whom affliction has touched and above all if the affliction is biological, is day-dreaming. It is the sole consolation, the unique resource of the afflicted; the one solace to help them bear the fearful burden of time; and a very innocent one, besides being indispensable. So how could it be possible to renounce it? It has only one disadvantage, which is that it is unreal. To renounce it for the love of truth is really to abandon all one's possessions in a mad excess of love and to follow him who is the personification of Truth. And it is really to bear the Cross; because time is the Cross.

While the limiting moment is still remote, it is not necessary to do this; but it is necessary to recognize day-dreaming for what it is. And even while one is sustained by it one must never forget for a moment that in all its forms — those that seem most inoffensive

by their childishness, those that seem most respectable by their seriousness and their connection with art or love or friendship — in
all its forms without exception, it is falsehood. It excludes Love.
Love is real.

I would never dare to speak to you like this if all these
thoughts were the product of my own mind. But although I am
unwilling to place any reliance on such impressions, I do really
have the feeling, in spite of myself, that God is addressing all this
to you, for love of you, through me. In the same way, it does
not matter if the consecrated host is made of the poorest quality
flour, not even if it is three parts rotten.

You say that I pay for my moral qualities by distrust of myself. But my attitude towards myself, which is not distrust but a
mixture of contempt and hatred and repulsion, is to be explained
on a lower level — on the level of biological mechanisms. For
twelve years I have suffered from pain around the central point
of the nervous system, the meeting-place of soul and body; this
pain persists during sleep and has never stopped for a second.
For a period of ten years it was so great, and was accompanied
by such exhaustion, that the effort of attention and intellectual
work was usually almost as despairing as that of a condemned
man the day before his execution, and often much more so, for
my efforts seemed completely sterile and without even any tem-
porary result. I was sustained by the faith, which I acquired at the
age of fourteen, that no true effort of attention is ever wasted,
even though it may never have any visible result, either direct
or indirect. Nevertheless, a time came when I thought my soul
menaced, through exhaustion and an aggravation of the pain, by
such a hideous and total breakdown that I spent several weeks
of anguished uncertainty whether death was not my imperative
duty — although it seemed to me appalling that my life should
end in horror. As I told you, I was only able to calm myself by
deciding to live conditionally, for a trial period.

A little earlier, when I had already been for years in this physical state, I worked for nearly a year in engineering factories in
the Paris region. The combination of personal experience and
sympathy for the wretched mass of people around me, in which

I formed, even in my own eyes, an undistinguishable item, implanted so deep in my heart the affliction of social degradation that I have felt a slave ever since, in the Roman sense of the word.

During all this time, the word "God" had no place at all in my thoughts. It never had, until the day — about three and a half years ago — when I could no longer keep it out. At a moment of intense physical pain, while I was making the effort to love, although believing I had no right to give any name to the love, I felt, while completely unprepared for it (I had never read the mystics), a presence more personal, more certain, and more real than that of a human being; it was inaccessible both to sense and to imagination, and it resembled the love that irradiates the tenderest smile of somebody one loves. Since that moment, the name of God and the name of Christ have been more and more irresistibly mingled with my thoughts.

Until then my only faith had been the Stoic *amor fati* as Marcus Aurelius understood it, and I had always faithfully practiced it — to love the universe as one's city; one's native country, the beloved fatherland of every soul; to cherish it for its beauty; in the total integrity of the order and necessity which are its substance, and all the events that occur in it.

The result was that the irreducible quantity of hatred and repulsion which goes with suffering and affliction recoiled entirely upon myself. And the quantity is very great, because the suffering in question is located at the very root of my every single thought, without exception.

This is so much the case that I absolutely cannot imagine the possibility that any human being could feel friendship for me. If I believe in yours it is only because I have confidence in you and you have assured me of it, so that my reason tells me to believe it. But this does not make it seem any the less impossible to my imagination.

Because of this propensity of my imagination I am all the more tenderly grateful to those who accomplish this impossibility. Because friendship is an incomparable, immeasurable boon to me, and a source of life — not metaphorically but literally. Since it is not only my body but my soul itself that is poisoned all through by suffering, it is impossible for my thought to dwell there and it is obliged to travel elsewhere. It can only dwell for brief moments in God; it dwells often among things; but it would be against nature for human thought never to dwell in anything human. Thus it is literally true that friendship gives to my thought all the life it has, apart from what comes to it from God or from the beauty of the world.

So you can see what you have done for me by giving me yours.

I say these things to you because you can understand them; for your last book contains a sentence, in which I recognize myself, about the mistake your friends make in thinking that you exist. That shows a type of sensibility which is only intelligible to those who experience existence directly and continuously as an evil. For them it is certainly very easy to do as Christ asks and deny themselves. Perhaps it is too easy. Perhaps it is without merit. And yet I believe that to have it made so easy is an immense privilege.

I am convinced that affliction on the one hand, and on the other hand joy, when it is a complete and pure commitment to perfect beauty, are the only two keys which give entry to the realm of purity, where one can breathe: the home of the real.

But each of them must be unmixed: the joy without a shadow of incompleteness, the affliction completely unconsoled.

You understand me, of course. That divine love which one touches in the depth of affliction, like Christ's resurrection through crucifixion, that love which is the central core and intangible essence of joy, is not a consolation. It leaves pain completely intact.

I am going to say something which is painful to think, more painful to say, and almost unbearably painful to say to those one loves. For anyone in affliction, evil can perhaps be defined as being everything that gives any consolation.

A pure joy, which in some cases may replace pain or in others may be superimposed on it, is not a consolation. On the other hand, there is often a consolation in morbidly aggravating one's pain. I don't know if I am expressing this properly; it is all quite clear to me.

The refuge of laziness and inertia, a temptation to which I succumb very often, almost every day, or I might say every hour, is a particularly despicable form of consolation. It compels me to despise myself.

I perceive that I have not answered your letter, and yet I have a lot to say about it. I must do it another time. Today I'll confine myself to thanking you for it.

Yours most truly,
S. Weil

I enclose the English poem, "Love," which I recited to you. It has played a big role in my life, because I was repeating it to myself at the moment when Christ came to take possession of me for the first time. I thought I was only reciting a beautiful poem but, unknown to me, it was a prayer.

THE LOVE OF GOD AND AFFLICTION

This is one of the most important of all Weil's essays. It was originally published in a shorter form. However, additional pages were later discovered, and are included here. This essay is the clearest exposition not only of affliction but also of Weil's understanding of the Cross, an understanding that comes through in almost everything she wrote in her last years.

In the realm of suffering, affliction is something apart, specific and irreducible. It is quite a different thing from simple suffering. It takes possession of the soul and marks it through and through with its own particular mark, the mark of slavery. Slavery as practiced by ancient Rome is simply the extreme form of affliction. The men of antiquity, who knew a lot about the subject, used to say: "A man loses half his soul the day he becomes a slave."

Affliction is inseparable from physical suffering and yet quite distinct. In suffering, all that is not bound up with physical pain or something analogous is artificial, imaginary, and can be eliminated by a suitable adjustment of the mind. Even in the case of the absence or death of someone we love, the irreducible part of the sorrow is akin to physical pain, a difficulty in breathing, a constriction of the heart, or an unsatisfied need, a hunger, or the almost biological disorder caused by the brutal unloosing of an energy hitherto absorbed by an attachment and now left undirected. A sorrow which is not centered around an irreducible core of such a nature is mere romanticism or literature. Humiliation is also a violent condition of the whole physical being, which wants to rise up against the outrage but is forced, by impotence or fear, to hold itself in check.

On the other hand a pain which is only physical is of very little account, and leaves no mark on the soul. Toothache is an example. An hour or two of violent pain caused by a bad tooth is nothing once it is over.

It is another matter if the physical suffering is very prolonged or frequent, but this is often something quite different from an attack of pain; it is often an affliction.

Affliction is an uprooting of life, a more or less attenuated equivalent of death, made irresistibly present to the soul by the attack or immediate apprehension of physical pain. If there is complete absence of physical pain there is no affliction for the soul, because thought can turn itself away in any direction. Thought flies from affliction as promptly and irresistibly as an animal flies from death. Here below, physical pain and nothing else has the power to chain down our thoughts; provided that we count as physical pain certain phenomena which, though difficult to describe, are bodily and are strictly equivalent to it; in particular, for example, the fear of physical pain.

When thought is obliged by an attack of physical pain, however slight, to recognize the presence of affliction, this produces a state of mind as acute as that of a condemned man who is forced to look for hours at the guillotine which is going to behead him. Human beings can live twenty years, fifty years, in this acute state. We pass by them without noticing. What man is capable of discerning them unless Christ himself looks through his eyes? We notice only that they sometimes behave strangely, and we censure this behavior.

There is not real affliction unless the event which has gripped and uprooted a life attacks it, directly or indirectly, in all its parts, social, psychological, and physical. The social factor is essential. There is not really affliction where there is not social degradation or the fear of it in some form or another.

There is both continuity and a separating threshold, like the boiling point of water, between affliction itself and all the sorrows which, even though they may be very violent, very deep, and very lasting, are not afflictions in the true sense. There is a limit; on the far side of it we have affliction but not on the near side. This limit is not purely objective; all sorts of personal factors have to be taken into account. The same event may plunge one human being into affliction and not another.

The great enigma of human life is not suffering but affliction. It is not surprising that the innocent are killed, tortured, driven from their country, made destitute or reduced to slavery, put in concentration camps or prison cells, since there are criminals to perform such actions. It is not surprising either that disease is the cause of long sufferings, which paralyze life and make it into an image of death, since nature is at the mercy of the blind play of mechanical necessities. But it is surprising that God should have given affliction the power to seize the very souls of the innocent and to possess them as sovereign master. At the very best, he who is branded by affliction will only keep half his soul.

As for those who have been struck the kind of blow which leaves the victim writhing on the ground like a half-crushed worm, they have no words to describe what is happening to them. Among the people they meet, those who have never had contact with affliction in its true sense can have no idea of what it is, even though they may have known much suffering. Affliction is something specific and impossible to compare with anything else, just as nothing can convey the idea of sound to the deaf and dumb. And, as for those who have themselves been mutilated by affliction, they are in no state to help anyone at all and are almost incapable of even wishing to do so. Thus compassion for the afflicted is an impossibility. When it is really found, it is a more astounding miracle than walking on water, healing the sick, or even raising the dead.

Affliction constrained Christ to implore that he might be spared, to seek consolation from man, to believe he was forsaken by the Father. It constrained a just man to cry out against God; a just man as perfect as human nature can be; more so, perhaps, if Job is not so much a historical character as a figure of Christ. "He laughs at the affliction of the innocent!" This is not blasphemy but a genuine cry of anguish. The Book of Job is a pure marvel of truth and authenticity from beginning to end. As regards affliction, all that departs from this model is more or less tainted with falsehood.

Affliction causes God to be absent for a time, more absent than a dead man, more absent than light in the utter darkness of a cell. A kind of horror submerges the whole soul. During this absence there is nothing to love. What is terrible is that if, in this darkness where there is nothing to love, the soul ceases to love, God's absence becomes final. The soul has to go on loving in the void, or at least to go on wanting to love, though it may be only with an infinitesimal part of itself. Then, one day, God will come to show himself to this soul and to reveal the beauty of the world to it, as in the case of Job. But if the soul stops loving it falls, even in this life, into something which is almost equivalent to hell.

That is why those who plunge men into affliction before they are prepared to receive it are killers of souls. On the other hand, in a time such as ours, where affliction is hanging over us all, help given to souls is effective only if it goes far enough really to prepare them for affliction. That is no small thing.

Affliction hardens and discourages because, like a red-hot iron, it stamps the soul to its very depths with the contempt, the disgust, and even the self-hatred and sense of guilt and defilement which crime logically should produce but actually does not. Evil dwells in the heart of the criminal without being felt there. It is felt in the heart of the man who is afflicted and innocent. Everything happens as though the state of soul appropriate for criminals had been separated from crime and attached to affliction; and it even seems to be in proportion to the innocence of those who are afflicted.

If Job cries out that he is innocent in such despairing accents it is because he himself is unable to believe so, it is because his soul within him is on the side of his friends. He implores God himself to bear witness, because he no longer hears the testimony of his own conscience; it is no longer anything but an abstract, lifeless memory for him.

Men have the same carnal nature as animals. If a hen is hurt, the others rush up and peck it. The phenomenon is as automatic as gravitation. Our senses attach to affliction all the contempt, all the revulsion, all the hatred which our reason attaches to crime. Except for those whose whole soul is inhabited by Christ, everybody despises the afflicted to some extent, although practically no one is conscious of it.

This law of sensibility also holds good with regard to ourselves. In the case of someone in affliction, all the contempt, revulsion, and hatred are turned inwards; they penetrate to the center of his soul and from there they color the whole universe with their poisoned light. Supernatural love, if it has survived, can prevent this second result from coming about, but not the first. The first is of the very essence of affliction; there is no affliction without it.

"Christ...being made a curse for us." It was not only the body of Christ, hanging on the wood, which was accursed; it was his whole soul also. In the same way every innocent being in his affliction feels himself accursed. This even goes on being true for those who have been in affliction and have come out of it through a change in their fortunes, if the affliction has bitten deeply enough into them.

Another effect of affliction is, little by little, to make the soul its accomplice, by injecting a poison of inertia into it. In anyone who has suffered affliction for a long enough time there is a complicity with regard to his own affliction. This complicity impedes all the efforts he might make to improve his lot; it goes so far as to prevent him from seeking a way of deliverance, sometimes even to the point of preventing him from wishing for deliverance. Then he is established in affliction, and people may get the impression that he is quite contented. Even worse, this complicity may induce him, in spite of himself, to shun and flee from the means of deliverance; and for this it will resort to pretexts which are sometimes ridiculous. Even after a man has been relieved of his affliction, there will be something left in him which impels him to embrace it again, if it has pierced irrevocably into the depth of his soul. It is as though affliction had established itself in him like a parasite and was directing him for its own purposes. Sometimes this impulse triumphs over all the impulses of the soul towards happiness. If the affliction has been ended as the result of some kindness, it may take the form of hatred for the benefactor; this is the cause of certain apparently inexplicable acts of savage ingratitude. It is sometimes easy to deliver an unhappy man from his present distress, but it is difficult to set him free from his past affliction. Only God can do it. And even the grace of God himself cannot cure irremediably wounded nature in this world. The glorified body of Christ bore the marks of nail and spear.

One can accept the existence of affliction only by considering it at a distance.

God created through love and for love. God did not create anything except love itself, and the means to love. He created love in all its forms. He created beings capable of love from all possible distances. Because no other could do it, he himself went to the greatest possible distance, the infinite distance. This infinite distance between God and God, this supreme tearing apart, this incomparable agony, this marvel of love, is the crucifixion. Nothing can be further from God than that which has been made accursed.

This tearing apart, over which supreme love places the bond of supreme union, echoes perpetually across the universe in the depth of the silence, like two notes, separate yet blending into one, like a pure and heartrending harmony. This is the Word of God. The whole creation is nothing but its vibration. When human music in its greatest purity pierces our soul, this is what we hear through it. When we have learned to hear the silence, this is what we grasp, even more distinctly, through it.

Those who persevere in love hear this note from the very lowest depths into which affliction has thrust them. From that moment they can no longer have any doubt.

Men struck down by affliction are at the foot of the Cross, almost at the greatest possible distance from God. It must not be thought that sin is a greater distance. Sin is not a distance; it is a turning of our eyes in the wrong direction.

It is true that there is a mysterious connection between this distance and an original disobedience. From the beginning, we are told, humanity turned its eyes away from God and walked as far as it could in the wrong direction. That is because it was then able to walk. As for us, we are nailed down to the spot, free only to choose which way we will look, ruled by necessity. A blind mechanism, heedless of degrees of spiritual perfection, continually buffets men hither and thither and flings some of them at the very foot of the Cross. It rests with them only to keep or not to keep their eyes turned towards God through all the shocks. It is not that God's Providence is absent; it is by his Providence that God willed necessity as a blind mechanism.

If the mechanism were not blind there would not be any affliction. Affliction is above all anonymous; it deprives its victims of their personality and turns them into things. It is indifferent, and it is the chill of this indifference — a metallic chill — which freezes all those it touches, down to the depth of their soul. They will never find warmth again. They will never again believe that they are anyone.

Affliction would not have this power without the element of chance which it contains. Those who are persecuted for their faith and are aware of it are not afflicted, in spite of their suffering. They fall into affliction only if suffering or fear fills the soul to the point of making it forget the cause of the persecution. The martyrs who came into the arena singing as they faced the wild beasts were not afflicted. Christ was afflicted. He did not die like a martyr. He died like a common criminal, in the same class as thieves, only a little more ridiculous. For affliction is ridiculous.

Only blind necessity can throw men to the extreme point of distance, close to the Cross. Human crime, which is the cause of most affliction, is part of blind necessity, because criminals do not know what they are doing.

There are two forms of friendship: meeting and separation. They are indissoluble. Both of them contain the same good, the unique good, which is friendship. For when two beings who are not friends are near each other there is no meeting, and when friends are far apart there is no separation. As both forms contain the same good thing, they are both equally good.

God produces himself and knows himself perfectly, just as we in our miserable way make and know objects outside ourselves. But, before all things, God is love. Before all things, God loves himself. This love, this friendship of God, is the Trinity. Between the terms united by this relation of divine love there is more than nearness; there is infinite nearness or identity. But through the creation, the Incarnation, and the Passion, there is also infinite distance. The interposed density of all space and all time sets an infinite distance between God and God.

Lovers or friends desire two things. The one is to love each other so much that they enter into each other and make only one being. The other is to love each other so much that, having half the globe between them, their union will not be diminished in the slightest degree. All that man vainly desires here below is perfectly realized in God. We have all those impossible desires within us as a mark of our destination, and they are good for us provided we no longer hope to fulfill them.

The love between God and God, which in itself *is* God, is this bond of double power; the bond which unites two beings so closely that they are no longer distinguishable and really form a single unity, and the bond which stretches across distance and triumphs over infinite separation. The unity of God, wherein all plurality disappears, and the abandonment wherein Christ believes he is left, while not ceasing to love his Father perfectly, these are two forms expressing the divine value of the same Love, the Love which is God himself.

God is so essentially love that the unity, which in a sense is his actual definition, is a pure effect of love. And corresponding to the infinite virtue of unification belonging to this love there is the infinite separation over which it triumphs, which is the whole creation spread throughout the totality of space and time, consisting of mechanically brutal matter and interposed between Christ and his Father.

As for us men, our misery gives us the infinitely precious privilege of sharing in this distance placed between the Son and his Father. This distance is only separation, however, for those who love. For those who love, separation, although painful, is a good, because it is love. Even the distress of the abandoned Christ is a good. There cannot be a greater good for us on earth than to share in it. God can never be perfectly present to us here below on account of our flesh. But he can be almost perfectly absent from us in extreme affliction. For us, on earth, this is the only possibility of perfection. That is why the Cross is our only hope. "No forest bears such a tree, with this flower, this foliage and this seed."

This universe where we are living, and of which we form a minute particle, is the distance put by the divine Love between God and God. We are a point in this distance. Space, time, and the mechanism that governs matter are the distance. Everything that we call evil is only this mechanism. God has provided that when his grace penetrates to the very center of a man and from there illuminates all his being, he is able to walk on the water without violating the laws of nature. But when a man turns away from God he simply gives himself up to the law of gravity. He then believes that he is deciding and choosing, but he is only a thing, a falling stone. If we examine human society and souls closely and with real attention, we see that wherever the virtue of supernatural light is absent, everything is obedient to mechanical laws as blind and as exact as the laws of gravitation. To know this is profitable and necessary. Those whom we call criminals are only tiles blown off a roof by the wind and falling at random. Their only fault is the initial choice by which they became those tiles.

The mechanism of necessity can be transposed on to any level while still remaining true to itself. It is the same in the world of blind matter, in plants, in animals, among nations, and in souls. Seen from our present standpoint, and in human perspective, it is quite blind. If, however, we transport our hearts beyond our-

selves, beyond the universe, beyond space and time, to where
our Father dwells, and if we regard this mechanism from there,
it appears quite different. What seemed to be necessity becomes
obedience. Matter is entirely passive and in consequence entirely
obedient to God's will. It is a perfect model for us. There cannot be any other being than God and that which obeys God.
On account of its perfect obedience, matter deserves to be loved
by those who love its Master, in the same way as a needle once
used by his beloved who has died is cherished by a lover. The
world's beauty gives us an intimation of its claim to a place in
our heart. In the beauty of the world harsh necessity becomes an
object of love. What is more beautiful than the effect of gravity
on sea waves as they flow in ever-changing folds, or the almost
eternal folds of the mountains?

The sea is not less beautiful in our eyes because we know that
ships are sometimes wrecked. On the contrary this adds to its
beauty. If it altered the movement of its waves to spare a ship it
would be a creature gifted with discernment and choice, and not
this fluid perfectly obedient to every external pressure. It is this
perfect obedience which makes the sea's beauty.

All the horrors which occur in this world are like the folds
imposed upon the waves by gravity. That is why they contain an
element of beauty. Sometimes a poem, such as the *Iliad,* makes
this beauty perceptible.

Men can never escape from obedience to God. A creature cannot but obey. The only choice given to men, as intelligent and
free creatures, is to desire obedience or not to desire it. If a man
does not desire it, he obeys all the same, perpetually, inasmuch
as he is a thing subject to mechanical necessity. If he does desire
it, he is still subject to mechanical necessity, but a new necessity
is added to it, a necessity constituted by the laws pertaining to
supernatural things. Certain actions become impossible for him;
others are accomplished by means of him, sometimes almost in
spite of himself.

When we have the feeling that on some occasion we have dis-
obeyed God, it simply means that we ceased for a time to desire
to be obedient. But of course, other things being equal, a man

does not perform the same actions if he gives his consent to obedience as if he does not; any more than a plant, other things being equal, grows in the same way if it is in the light as if it is in the dark. The plant does not have any control or choice in the matter of its own growth. We, however, are like plants which have the one choice of being in or out of the light.

Christ proposed the docility of matter to us as a model when he told us to consider the lilies of the field which neither toil nor spin. This means that they did not set out to clothe themselves in such or such a color, they have not exercised their will nor made arrangements for such a purpose, they have received everything that natural necessity brought them. If they seem to us infinitely more beautiful than the richest stuffs, it is not because they are richer but because of their docility. Materials are docile too, but docile to man, not to God. Matter is not beautiful when it obeys man, but only when it obeys God. If sometimes in a work of art it seems almost as beautiful as in the sea or in mountains or in flowers it is because the light of God has filled the artist. In order to find beautiful those things which are made by men unenlightened by God, it is necessary to have understood with all one's soul that these men themselves are only matter which obeys without knowing it. For anyone who has reached this point, absolutely everything here below is perfectly beautiful. In everything which exists, in everything which happens, he discerns the mechanism of necessity and he recognizes in this necessity the infinite sweetness of obedience. For us, this obedience of things in relation to God is what the transparency of a window pane is in relation to light. As soon as we feel this obedience with our whole being, we see God.

When we hold a newspaper upside down, we see the odd shapes of the printed characters. When we turn it the right way up, we no longer see the characters, we see words. The passenger on a ship in a storm feels each shock as an inward upheaval. The captain is aware only of the complex combination of wind, current, and swell, with the ship's position and its shape, its sails, and its helm.

As one has to learn to read, or to practice a trade, so one must

learn to feel in all things, first and almost solely, the obedience of
the universe to God. It is truly an apprenticeship; and like every
apprenticeship it calls for time and effort. For the man who has
finished his training the differences between things or between
events are no more important than those perceived by someone
who knows how to read when he has before him the same sentence repeated several times, in red ink and blue, and printed in
this, that, and the other kind of type. The man who cannot read
sees only the differences. For the man who can read it all comes
to the same thing, because the sentence is the same. Whoever has
finished his apprenticeship recognizes things and events, everywhere and always, as vibrations of the same divine and infinitely
sweet word. Which is not to say that he will not suffer. Pain is
the color of certain events. When a man who can and a man who
cannot read look at a sentence written in red ink they both see
something red; but the red color is not so important for the one
as for the other.

When an apprentice gets hurt or complains of fatigue, workmen and peasants have this fine expression: "It's the trade getting
into his body." Whenever we have some pain to endure, we can
say to ourselves that it is the universe, the order and beauty of the
world, and the obedience of creation to God which are entering
our body. After that how can we fail to bless with the tenderest
gratitude the Love which sends us this gift?

Joy and suffering are two equally precious gifts which must
both of them be fully tasted, each one in its purity and without
trying to mix them. Through joy, the beauty of the world penetrates our soul. Through suffering it penetrates our body. We
could no more become friends of God through joy alone than
one becomes a ship's captain by studying books on navigation.
The body plays a part in all apprenticeships. On the plane of
physical sensibility, suffering alone gives us contact with that necessity which constitutes the order of the world, for pleasure does
not involve an impression of necessity. It is on a higher plane of
sensibility that the necessity in joy can be recognized, and then
only indirectly through the sense of beauty. In order that our being may one day become wholly sensitive in every part to this

obedience which is the substance of matter, in order that a new sense may be formed in us which allows us to hear the universe as the vibration of the word of God, the transforming power of suffering and joy are equally indispensable. When either of them comes to us we have to open the very center of our soul to it, as a woman opens her door to messengers from her beloved. What does it matter to a lover if the messenger is courteous or rough so long as he gives her a message?

But affliction is not suffering. Affliction is something quite different from a divine educational method.

The infinity of space and time separates us from God. How can we seek for him? How can we go towards him? Even if we were to walk for endless centuries we should do no more than go round and round the world. Even in an airplane we could not do anything else. We are incapable of progressing vertically. We cannot take one step towards the heavens. God crosses the universe and comes to us.

Over the infinity of space and time the infinitely more infinite love of God comes to possess us. He comes at his own time. We have the power to consent to receive him or to refuse. If we remain deaf he comes back again and again a beggar, but also, like a beggar, one day he stops coming. If we consent, God places a little seed in us and he goes away again. From that moment God has no more to do; neither have we, except to wait. We have only not to regret the consent we gave, the nuptial Yes. It is not as easy as it seems, for the growth of the seed within us is painful. Moreover, from the very fact that we accept this growth we cannot avoid destroying whatever gets in its way, pulling up the weeds, cutting the grasses; and unfortunately they are part of our very flesh, so that this gardening amounts to a violent operation. On the whole, however, the seed grows of itself. A day comes when the soul belongs to God, when it not only consents to love but when truly and effectively it loves. Then in its turn it must cross the universe to go to God. The soul does not love like a creature, with created love. The love within it is divine, uncreated, for it is the love of God for God which is passing through it. God alone is capable of loving God. We can only consent to give up our own feelings so as to allow free passage in our soul for this love. That is the meaning of denying oneself. We were created solely in order to give this consent.

The divine Love crossed the infinity of space and time to come from God to us. But how can it repeat the journey in the opposite direction, starting from a finite creature? When the seed of divine love placed in us has grown and become a tree, how can we, we who bear it, take it back to its origin? How can we make, in the opposite direction, the journey which God made when he came to us? How can we cross infinite distance?

It seems impossible, but there is a way. It is a way well known to us. We are quite well aware of the likeness in which this tree is made, this tree which has grown within us, this most beautiful tree where the birds of the air come and perch. We know what is the most beautiful of all trees. "No forest bears its equal." Something even a little more frightful than a gallows — that is the most beautiful of all trees. It was the seed of this tree that God placed within us, without our knowing what seed it was. If we had known, we should not have said Yes at the first moment. It is this tree which has grown within us and which has become ineradicable. Only a betrayal could uproot it.

When a hammer strikes a nail the shock travels, without losing any of its force, from the nail's large head to the point, although it is only a point. If the hammer and the nail's head were infinitely large the effect would still be the same. The point of the nail would transmit this infinite shock at the place where it was applied.

Extreme affliction, which means physical pain, distress of soul, and social degradation, all together, is the nail. The point of the nail is applied to the very center of the soul, and its head is the whole of necessity throughout all space and time.

Affliction is a marvel of divine technique. It is a simple and ingenious device to introduce into the soul of a finite creature that immensity of force, blind, brutal, and cold. The infinite distance which separates God from the creature is concentrated into a point to transfix the center of a soul.

The man to whom such a thing occurs has no part in the operation. He quivers like a butterfly pinned alive to a tray. But throughout the horror he can go on wanting to love. There is no impossibility in that, no obstacle, one could almost say no difficulty. Because no pain, however great, up to the point of losing consciousness, touches that part of the soul which consents to a right orientation.

It is only necessary to know that love is an orientation and not a state of the soul. Anyone who does not know this will fall into despair at the first onset of affliction.

The man whose soul remains oriented towards God while a nail is driven through it finds himself nailed to the very center of the universe; the true center, which is not in the middle, which is not in space and time, which is God. In a dimension which is not spatial and which is not time, a totally other dimension, the nail has pierced through the whole of creation, through the dense screen which separates the soul from God.

In this marvelous dimension, without leaving the time and place to which the body is bound, the soul can traverse the whole of space and time and come into the actual presence of God.

It is at the point of intersection between creation and Creator. This point is the point of intersection of the two branches of the Cross.

St. Paul was perhaps thinking about things of this kind when he said: "That ye, being rooted and grounded in love, may be able to comprehend with all saints what is the breadth, and length, and depth, and height; and to know the love of Christ, which passeth knowledge."

If the tree of life, and not simply the divine seed, is already formed in a man's soul at the time when extreme affliction strikes him, then he is nailed to the same Cross as Christ.

Otherwise, there is the choice between the crosses on each side of Christ's.

We are like the impenitent thief if we seek consolation in contempt and hatred for our fellows in misfortune. This is the commonest effect of real affliction; it was so in the case of Roman slavery. People who are surprised when they observe such a state of mind in the afflicted would almost all fall into it themselves if affliction struck them.

To be like the good thief it is sufficient to remember that no matter what degree of affliction one is submerged in, one has deserved at least that much. Because it is certain that before being reduced to impotence by affliction one has been an accomplice, through cowardice, inertia, indifference, or culpable ignorance, in crimes which have plunged other human beings into an affliction at least as great. Generally, no doubt, we could not prevent those crimes, but we could express our reprobation of them. We neglected to do so, or even approved them, or at least we concurred in the expression of approval around us. For this complicity, the affliction we are suffering is not, in strict justice, too great a penalty. We have no right to feel compassion for ourselves. We know that at least once a perfectly innocent being suffered a worse affliction; it is better to direct our compassion to him across the centuries.

That is what everybody can and ought to say to himself. Because among our institutions and customs there are things so atrocious that nobody can legitimately feel himself innocent of this diffused complicity. It is certain that each of us is involved at least in the guilt of criminal indifference.

But in addition it is the right of every man to desire to have his part in Christ's own Cross. We have an unlimited right to ask God for everything that is good. In such demands there is no need for humility or moderation.

It is wrong to desire affliction, it is against nature, and it is a perversion, and moreover it is the essence of affliction that it is suffered unwillingly. So long as we are not submerged in affliction all we can do is to desire that, if it should come, it may be a participation in the Cross of Christ.

But what is in fact always present, and what it is therefore always permitted to love, is the possibility of affliction. All the three sides of our being are always exposed to it. Our flesh is fragile; it can be pierced or torn or crushed, or one of its internal mechanisms can be permanently deranged, by any piece of matter in motion. Our soul is vulnerable, being subject to fits of depression without cause and pitifully dependent upon all sorts of objects, inanimate and animate, which are themselves fragile and capricious. Our social personality, upon which our sense of existence almost depends, is always and entirely exposed to every hazard. These three parts of us are linked with the very center of our being in such a way that it bleeds for any wound of the slightest consequence which they suffer. Above all, anything which diminishes or destroys our social prestige, our right to consideration, seems to impair or abolish our very essence — so much is our whole substance an affair of illusion.

When everything is going more or less well, we do not think about this almost infinite fragility. But nothing compels us not to think about it. We can contemplate it all the time and thank God for it unceasingly. We can be thankful not only for the fragility itself but also for that more intimate weakness which connects it with the very center of our being. For it is this weakness which makes possible, in certain conditions, the operation by which we are nailed to the very center of the Cross.

We can think of this fragility, with love and gratitude, on the occasion of any suffering, whether great or small. We can think of it at times when we are neither particularly happy nor unhappy. We can think of it whenever we experience any joy. This, however, we ought not to do if the thought were liable to cloud or lessen the joy. But it is not so. This thought only adds a more piercing sweetness to joy, in the same way that the flowers of the cherry are the more beautiful for being frail.

If we dispose our thought in this way, then after a certain time the Cross of Christ should become the very substance of our life. No doubt this is what Christ meant when he advised his friends to bear their cross each day, and not, as people seem to think nowadays, simply that one should be resigned about one's little daily troubles — which, by an almost sacrilegious abuse of language, people sometimes refer to as crosses. There is only one cross; it is the whole of that necessity by which the infinity of space and time is filled and which, in given circumstances, can be concentrated upon the atom that any one of us is, and totally pulverize it. To bear one's cross is to bear the knowledge that one is entirely subject to this blind necessity in every part of one's being, except for one point in the soul which is so secret that it is inaccessible to consciousness. However cruelly a man suffers, if there is some part of his being still intact and if he is not fully conscious that it has escaped only by chance and remains every moment at the mercy of chance, he has no part in the Cross. This is above all the case when the part of the soul which remains intact, or even relatively intact, is the social part; which is the reason why sickness profits nothing unless there is added to it the spirit of poverty in its perfection. It is possible for a perfectly happy man — if he recognizes, truly, concretely, and all the time, the possibility of affliction — to enjoy happiness completely and at the same time bear his cross.

But it is not enough to be aware of this possibility; one must love it. One must tenderly love the harshness of that necessity which is like a coin with two faces, the one turned towards us being domination, and the one turned towards God, obedience. We must embrace it closely even if it offers its roughest surface and the roughness cuts into us. Any lover is glad to clasp tightly some object belonging to an absent loved one, even to the point where it cuts into the flesh. We know that this universe is an object belonging to God. We ought to thank God from the depth of our hearts for giving us necessity, his mindless, sightless, and perfectly obedient slave, as absolute sovereign. She drives us with a whip. But being subject in this world to her tyranny, we have only to choose God for our treasure, and put our heart with it, and from that moment we shall see the other face of the tyranny, the face which is pure obedience. We are the slaves of necessity, but we are also the sons of her Master. Whatever she demands of us, we ought to love the sight of her docility, we who are the children of the house. When she does not do as we wish, when she compels us to suffer what we would not, it is given us by means of love to pass through to the other side and to see the face of obedience which she turns towards God. Lucky are those to whom this precious opportunity comes often.

Intense and long-drawn-out physical pain has this unique advantage, that our sensibility is so made as to be unable to accept it. We can get used to, make the best of, and adapt ourselves to anything else except that; and we make the adaptation, in order to have the illusion of power, in order to believe that we are in control. We play at imagining that we have chosen what is forced upon us. But when a human being is transformed, in his own eyes, into a sort of animal, almost paralyzed and altogether repulsive, he can no longer retain that illusion. It is all the better if this transformation is brought about by human wills, as a result of social reprobation, provided that it is not an honorable persecution but, as it were, a blind, anonymous oppression. In its physical part, the soul is aware of necessity only as constraint and is aware of constraints only as pain. It is the same truth which penetrates into the senses through pain, into the intelligence through mathematical proof, and into the faculty of love through beauty. So it was that to Job, when once the veil of flesh had been rent by affliction, the world's stark beauty was revealed. The beauty of the world appears when we recognize that the substance of the universe is necessity and that the substance of necessity is obedience to a perfectly wise Love. The universe of which we are a fraction has no other essence than to be obedient.

In the joy of the senses there is a virtue analogous to that of physical pain, if the joy is so vivid and pure, if it so far exceeds expectation that we immediately recognize our inability to procure anything like it, or to retain its possession, by our own efforts. Of such joys, beauty is always the essence. Pure joy and pure pain are two aspects of the same infinitely precious truth. Fortunately so, because it is this that gives us the right to wish joy rather than pain to those we love.

The Trinity and the Cross are the two poles of Christianity, the two essential truths: the first, perfect joy; the second, perfect affliction. It is necessary to know both the one and the other and their mysterious unity, but the human condition in this world places us infinitely far from the Trinity, at the very foot of the Cross. Our country is the Cross.

The knowledge of affliction is the key of Christianity. But that knowledge is impossible. It is not possible to know affliction without having been through it. Thought is so revolted by affliction that it is as incapable of bringing itself voluntarily to conceive it as an animal, generally speaking, is incapable of suicide. Thought never knows affliction except by constraint. Unless constrained by experience, it is impossible to believe that everything in the soul — all its thoughts and feelings, its very attitude towards ideas, people, and the universe, and, above all, the most intimate attitude of the being towards itself — that all this is entirely at the mercy of circumstances. Even if one recognizes it theoretically, and it is rare indeed to do so, one does not believe it with all one's soul. To believe it with all one's soul is what Christ called, not renunciation or abnegation, as it is usually translated, but denying oneself; and it is by this that one deserves to be his disciple. But when we are in affliction or have passed through it we do not believe this truth any more than before; one could almost say that we believe it still less. Thought can never really be constrained; evasion by falsehood is always open to it. When thought finds itself, through the force of circumstance, brought face to face with affliction it takes immediate refuge in lies, like a hunted animal dashing for cover. Sometimes in its terror it burrows very deep into falsehood and it often happens that people who are or have been in affliction become addicted to lying as a vice, in some cases to such a degree that they lose the sense of any distinction between truth and falsehood in anything. It is wrong to blame them. Falsehood and affliction are so closely linked that Christ conquered the world simply because he, being the Truth, continued to be the Truth in the very depth of extreme affliction. Thought is constrained by an instinct of self-preservation to fly from the sight of affliction, and this instinct is infinitely more essential to our being than the instinct to avoid physical death. It is comparatively easy to face physical death so long as circumstances or the play of imagination present it under some other aspect than that of affliction. But to be able to face affliction with steady attention when it is close to him a man must be prepared, for the love of truth, to accept the death of the soul. This is the death of which Plato spoke when he said "to philosophize is to learn to die"; it is the death which was symbolized in the initiation rites of the ancient mysteries, and which is represented by baptism. In reality, it is not a question of the soul's dying, but simply of recognizing the truth that it is a dead thing, something analogous to matter. It has no need to turn into water; it is water; the thing we believe to be our self is as ephemeral and automatic a product of external circumstances as the form of a sea-wave.

It is only necessary to know that, to know it in the depth of one's being. But to know humanity in that way belongs to God alone and to those in this world who have been regenerated from on high. For it is impossible to accept that death of the soul unless one possesses another life in addition to the soul's illusory life, unless one has placed one's treasure and one's heart elsewhere — and not merely outside one's person but outside all one's thoughts and feelings and outside everything knowable, in the hands of our Father who is in secret. Of those who have done this one can say that they have been born of water and the Spirit; for they are no longer anything except a twofold obedience — on the one side to the mechanical necessity in which their earthly condition involves them, and on the other to the divine inspiration. There is nothing left in them which one could call their own will, their person, their "I." They have become nothing other than a certain intersection of nature and God. This intersection is the name with which God has named them from all eternity; it is their vocation. In the old baptism by immersion the man disappeared under the water; this means to deny one's self, to acknowledge that one is only a fragment of the inert matter which is the fabric of creation. He only reappeared because he was lifted up by an ascending movement stronger than gravity; this is the image of the divine love in man. Baptism contains the symbol of the state of perfection. The engagement it involves is the promise to desire that state and to beseech God for it, incessantly and untiringly, for as long as one has not obtained it — as a hungry child never stops asking his father for bread. But we cannot know what this promise commits us to until we encounter the terrible presence of affliction. It is only there, face to face with affliction, that the true commitment can be made, through a more secret, more mysterious, more miraculous contact even than a sacrament.

The knowledge of affliction being by nature impossible both to those who have experienced it and to those who have not, it is equally possible for both of them by supernatural favor, other-

wise Christ would not have spared from affliction the man he
cherished above all, and after having promised that he should
drink from his cup. In both cases the knowledge of affliction is
something much more miraculous than walking on water.

Those whom Christ recognized as his benefactors are those
whose compassion rested upon the knowledge of affliction. The
others give capriciously, irregularly, or else too regularly, or from
habit imposed by training, or in conformity with social conven-
tion, or from vanity or emotional pity, or for the sake of a good
conscience — in a word, from self-regarding motives. They are
arrogant or patronizing or tactlessly sympathetic, or they let the
afflicted man feel that they regard him simply as a specimen of a
certain type of affliction. In any case, their gift is an injury. And
they have their reward on earth, because their left hand is not
unaware of what their right hand gave. Their contact with the
afflicted must be a false one because the true understanding of
the afflicted implies knowledge of affliction. Those who have not
seen the face of affliction, or are not prepared to, can only approach the afflicted behind a veil of illusion or falsehood. If the
look of affliction itself is revealed by chance on the face of the
afflicted, they run away.

The benefactor of Christ, when he meets an afflicted man, does
not feel any distance between himself and the other. He projects
all his own being into him. It follows that the impulse to give
him food is as instinctive and immediate as it is for oneself to
eat when one is hungry. And it is forgotten almost at once, just
as one forgets yesterday's meals. Such a man would not think of
saying that he takes care of the afflicted for the Lord's sake; it
would seem as absurd to him as it would be to say that he eats
for the Lord's sake. One eats because one can't help it. Christ will
thank the people who give in the way they eat.

They do for the afflicted something very different from feeding,
clothing, or taking care of them. By projecting their own being
into those they help they give them for a moment — what affliction has deprived them of — an existence of their own. Affliction
is essentially a destruction of personality, a lapse into anonymity.
Just as Christ put off his divinity for love, so the afflicted are

stripped of their humanity by misfortune. In affliction, that misfortune itself becomes a man's whole existence and in every other respect he loses all significance, in everybody's eyes including his own. There is something in him that would like to exist, but it is continually pushed back into nothingness, like a drowning man whose head is pushed under the water. He may be a pauper, a refugee, a Negro, an invalid, an ex-convict, or anything of the kind; in any case, whether he is an object of ill usage or of charity he will in either case be treated as a cipher, as one item among many others in the statistics of a certain type of affliction. So both good treatment and bad treatment will have the same effect of compelling him to remain anonymous. They are two forms of the same offense.

The man who sees someone in affliction and projects into him his own being brings to birth in him through love, at least for a moment, an existence apart from his affliction. For, although affliction is the occasion of this supernatural process, it is not the cause. The cause is the identity of human beings across all the apparent distances placed between them by the hazards of fortune.

To project one's being into an afflicted person is to assume for a moment his affliction, it is to choose voluntarily something whose very essence consists in being imposed by constraints upon the unwilling. And that is an impossibility. Only Christ has done it. Only Christ and those men whose whole soul he possesses can do it. What these men give to the afflicted whom they succor, when they project their own being into them, is not really their own being, because they no longer possess one; it is Christ himself.

Charity like this is a sacrament, a supernatural process by which a man in whom Christ dwells really puts Christ into the soul of the afflicted. If it is bread that is given, this bread is equivalent to the host. And this is not speaking symbolically or by conjecture; it is a literal translation of Christ's own words. He says: "You have done it unto me." Therefore he is in the naked or starving man. But he is not there in virtue of the nakedness or hunger, because affliction in itself contains no gift from above. Therefore Christ's presence can only be due to the operation of charity. It is obvious that Christ is in the man whose charity is perfectly pure; for who could be Christ's benefactor except Christ himself? And it is easy to understand that only Christ's presence in a soul can put true compassion in it. But the Gospel reveals further that he who gives from true compassion gives Christ himself. The afflicted who receive this miraculous gift have the choice of consenting to it or not.

In affliction, if it is complete, a man is deprived of all human relationship. For him there are only two possible kinds of relation with men: the first, in which he figures only as a thing, is as mechanical as the relation between two contiguous drops of water, and the second is purely supernatural love. All relationships between these two extremes are forbidden him. There is no place in his life for anything except water and the Spirit. Affliction, when it is consented to and accepted and loved, is truly a baptism.

It is because Christ alone is capable of compassion that he received none while he was on earth. Being in the flesh in this world, he was not at the same time in the souls of those around him; and so there was no one to have pity on him. When suffering compelled him to seek pity, his closest friends refused it; they left him to suffer alone. Even John slept; and Peter, who had been able to walk on water, was incapable of pity when his master fell into affliction. So as to avoid seeing him, they took refuge in sleep. When Pity herself becomes affliction, where can she turn for help? It would have needed another Christ to have pity on Christ in affliction. In the centuries that followed, pity for Christ's affliction was one of the signs of sanctity.

The supernatural process of charity, as opposed to that of communion, for example, does not need to be completely conscious. Those whom Christ thanks reply: "Lord, when...?" They did not know whom they were feeding. In general, there is nothing even to show that they knew anything at all about Christ. They may or they may not have. The important thing is that they were just; and because of that the Christ within them gave himself in the form of almsgiving. Beggars are fortunate people, in that there is a possibility of their receiving once or twice in their life such an alms.

Affliction is truly at the center of Christianity. Through it is accomplished the sole and twofold commandment: "Love God," "Love your neighbor." For, as regards the first, it was said by Christ: "No man cometh unto the Father, but by me"; and he also said: "As Moses lifted up the serpent in the wilderness, even so must the Son of man be lifted up: that whosoever believeth in him should not perish, but have eternal life." The serpent is that serpent of bronze which it was sufficient to look upon to be saved from the effects of poison. Therefore it is only by looking upon the Cross that we can love God. And as regards our neighbor, Christ has said who is the neighbor whom we are commanded to love. It is the naked, bleeding, and senseless body which we see lying in the road. What we are commanded to love first of all is affliction: the affliction of man, the affliction of God.

People often reproach Christianity for a morbid preoccupation with suffering and grief. This is an error. Christianity is not concerned with suffering and grief, for they are sensations, psychological states, in which a perverse indulgence is always possible; its concern is with something quite different, which is affliction. Affliction is not a psychological state; it is a pulverization of the soul by the mechanical brutality of circumstances. The transformation of a man, in his own eyes, from the human condition into that of a half-crushed worm writhing on the ground is a process which not even a pervert would find attractive. Neither does it attract a sage, a hero, or a saint. Affliction is something which imposes itself upon a man quite against his will. Its essence, the thing it is defined by, is the horror, the revulsion of the whole being, which it inspires in its victim. And this is the very thing one must consent to, by virtue of supernatural love.

It is our function in this world to consent to the existence of the universe. God is not satisfied with finding his creation good; he wants it also to find itself good. That is the purpose of the souls which are attached to minute fragments of this world; and it is the purpose of affliction to provide the occasion for judging that God's creation is good. Because, so long as the play of circumstance around us leaves our being almost intact, or only half impaired, we more or less believe that the world is created and controlled by ourselves. It is affliction that reveals, suddenly and to our very great surprise, that we are totally mistaken. After that, if we praise, it is really God's creation that we are praising. And where is the difficulty? We are well aware that divine glory is in no way diminished by our affliction; therefore we are in no way prevented from praising God for his great glory.

Thus, affliction is the surest sign that God wishes to be loved by us; it is the most precious evidence of his tenderness. It is something altogether different from a paternal chastisement, and could more justly be compared to the tender quarrels by which a young couple confirm the depth of their love. We dare to look affliction in the face; otherwise we should see after a little time that it is the face of love. In the same way Mary Magdalene perceived that he whom she took to be the gardener was someone else.

Seeing the central position occupied in their faith by affliction, Christians ought to suspect that it is in a sense the very essence of creation. To be a created thing is not necessarily to be afflicted, but it is necessarily to be exposed to affliction. Only the uncreated is indestructible. Those who ask why God permits affliction might as well as why God created. And that, indeed, is a question one may well ask. Why did God create? It seems so obvious that God is greater than God and the creation together. At least, it seems obvious so long as one thinks of God as Being. But that is not how one ought to think of him. So soon as one thinks of God as Love one senses that marvel of love by which the Father and the Son are united both in the eternal unity of the one God and also across the separating distance of space and time and the Cross.

God is love, and nature is necessity; but this necessity, through obedience, is a mirror of love. In the same way, God is joy, and creation is affliction; but it is an affliction radiant with the light of joy. Affliction contains the truth about our condition. They alone will see God who prefer to recognize the truth and die, instead of living a long and happy existence in a state of illusion. One must want to go towards reality; then, when one thinks one has found a corpse, one meets an angel who says: "He is risen."

The Cross of Christ is the only source of light that is bright enough to illumine affliction. Wherever there is affliction, in any age or any country, the Cross of Christ is the truth of it. Any man, whatever his beliefs may be, has his part in the Cross of Christ if he loves truth to the point of facing affliction rather than escape into the depths of falsehood. If God had been willing to withhold Christ from the men of any given country or epoch, we should know it by an infallible sign; there would be no affliction among them. We know of no such period in history. Wherever there is affliction there is the Cross — concealed, but present to anyone who chooses truth rather than falsehood and love rather than hate. Affliction without the Cross is hell, and God has not placed hell upon the earth.

Conversely, there are many Christians who have no part in Christ because they lack the strength to recognize and worship the blessed Cross in every affliction. There is no such proof of feebleness of faith as the way in which people, even including Christians, sidetrack the problem of affliction when they discuss it. All the talk about original sin, God's will, Providence and its mysterious plans (which nevertheless one thinks one can try to fathom), and future recompenses of every kind in this world and the next, all this only serves to conceal the reality of affliction, or else fails to meet the case. There is only one thing that enables us to accept real affliction, and that is the contemplation of Christ's Cross. There is nothing else. That one thing suffices.

A mother, a wife, or a fiancée, if they know that the person they love is in distress, will want to help him and be with him, and if that is impossible they will at least seek to lessen their distance from him and lighten the heavy burden of impotent sympathy by suffering some equivalent distress. Whoever loves Christ and thinks of him on the Cross should feel a similar relief when gripped by affliction.

By reason of the essential link between the Cross and affliction, no State has the right to dissociate itself from all religion except on the absurd hypothesis that it has succeeded in abolishing affliction. *A fortiori* it has no such right if it is itself creating affliction. A penal system entirely disassociated from any reference to God has a really infernal aura. Not on account of wrong verdicts or excessive punishments but, apart from all that, in it-self. It defiles itself by contact with every defilement, and since it contains no purifying principle it becomes so polluted that it can further degrade even the most degraded criminal. Contact with it is hideous for anyone with any integrity or health of mind; and, as for the corrupt, they find an even more horribly corrupt sort of appeasement in the very punishment it inflicts. Nothing is pure enough to bring purity to the places reserved for crime and punishment except Christ, who was himself condemned by the law.

But it is only the Cross, and not the complications of dogma, that is needed by States; and it is disastrous that the Cross and dogma have become so closely linked. By this link, Christ has been drawn away from the criminals who are his brothers.

The idea of necessity as the material common to art, science, and every kind of labor is the door by which Christianity can enter profane life and permeate the whole of it. For the Cross is necessity itself brought into contact with the lowest and the highest part of us; with our physical sensibility by its evocation of physical pain and with supernatural love by the presence of God. It thus involves the whole range of contacts with necessity which are possible for the intermediate parts of our being.

There is not, there cannot be, any human activity in whatever sphere, of which Christ's Cross is not the supreme and secret truth. No activity can be separated from it without rotting or shriveling like a cut vine-shoot. That is what is happening to-day, before our uncomprehending eyes, while we ask ourselves what has gone wrong. And Christians comprehend least of all because, knowing that the roots of our activities go back long be-fore Christ, they cannot understand that the Christian faith is the sap in them.

But this would be no problem if we understood that the Chris-tian faith, under veils which do not obscure its radiance, comes to flower and fruit at every time and every place where there are men who do not hate the light.

Never since the dawn of history, except for a certain period of the Roman Empire, has Christ been so absent as today. The separation of religion from the rest of social life, which seems natural even to the majority of Christians nowadays, would have been judged monstrous by antiquity.

The sap of Christianity should be made to flow everywhere in the life of society; but nevertheless it is destined above all for man in solitude. The Father is in secret, and there is no secret more inviolable than affliction.

There is a question which is absolutely meaningless and therefore, of course, unanswerable, and which we normally never ask ourselves, but in affliction the soul is constrained to repeat it incessantly like a sustained, monotonous groan. This question is: Why? Why are things as they are? The afflicted man naively seeks an answer, from men, from things, from God, even if he disbelieves in him, from anything or everything. Why is it necessary precisely that he should have nothing to eat, or be worn out with fatigue and brutal treatment, or be about to be executed, or be ill, or be in prison? If one explained to him the causes which have produced his present situation, and this is in any case seldom possible because of the complex interaction of circumstances, it will not seem to him to be an answer. For his question "Why?" does not mean "By what cause?" but "For what purpose?" And it is impossible, of course, to indicate any purposes to him; unless we invent some imaginary ones, but that sort of invention is not a good thing.

It is singular that the affliction of other people, except sometimes, though not always, those very close to us, does not provoke this question. At the most, it may occur to us casually for a moment. But so soon as a man falls into affliction the question takes hold and goes on repeating itself incessantly. Why? Why? Christ himself asked it: "Why hast thou forsaken me?"

There can be no answer to the "Why?" of the afflicted, because the world is necessity and not purpose. If there were finality in the world, the place of the good would not be in the other world. Whenever we look for final causes in this world it refuses them. But to know that it refuses, one has to ask.

The only things that compel us to ask the question are affliction, and also beauty; for the beautiful gives us such a vivid sense of the presence of something good that we look for some purpose

there, without ever finding one. Like affliction, beauty compels us
to ask: Why? Why is this thing beautiful? But rare are those who
are capable of asking themselves this question for as long as a few
hours at a time. The afflicted man's question goes on for hours,
days, years; it ceases only when he has no strength left.

He who is capable not only of crying out but also of listening
will hear the answer. Silence is the answer. This is the eternal
silence for which Vigny bitterly reproached God; but Vigny had
no right to say how the just man should reply to the silence, for
he was not one of the just. The just man loves. He who is capable
not only of listening but also of loving hears this silence as the
word of God.

The speech of created beings is with sounds. The word of
God is silence. God's secret word of love can be nothing else but
silence. Christ is the silence of God.

Just as there is no tree like the Cross, so there is no harmony
like the silence of God. The Pythagoreans discerned this harmony
in the fathomless eternal silence around the stars. In this world,
necessity is the vibration of God's silence.

Our soul is constantly clamorous with noise, but there is one
point in it which is silence, and which we never hear. When the
silence of God comes to the soul and penetrates it and joins the
silence which is secretly present in us, from then on we have our
treasure and our heart in God; and space opens before us as the
opening fruit of a plant divides in two, for we are seeing the
universe from a point situated outside space.

This operation can take place in only two ways, to the exclu-
sion of all others. There are only two things piercing enough to
penetrate our souls in this way; they are affliction and beauty.

Often, one could weep tears of blood to think how many
unfortunates are crushed by affliction without knowing how to
make use of it. But, coolly considered, this is not a more pitiful
waste than the squandering of the world's beauty. The brightness of stars, the sound of sea-waves, the silence of the hour
before dawn — how often do they not offer themselves in vain
to men's attention? To pay no attention to the world's beauty is,
perhaps, so great a crime of ingratitude that it deserves the pun-

ishment of affliction. To be sure, it does not always get it; but then the alternative punishment is a mediocre life, and in what way is a mediocre life preferable to affliction? Moreover, even in the case of great misfortune such people's lives are probably still mediocre. So far as conjecture is possible about sensibility, it would seem that the evil within a man is a protection against the external evil that attacks him in the form of pain. One must hope it is so, and that for the impenitent thief God has mercifully reduced to insignificance such useless suffering. In fact, it certainly is so, because that is the great temptation which affliction offers; it is always possible for an afflicted man to suffer less by consenting to become wicked.

The man who has known pure joy, if only for a moment, and who has therefore tasted the flavor of the world's beauty, for it is the same thing, is the only man for whom affliction is something devastating. At the same time, he is the only man who has not deserved this punishment. But, after all, for him it is no punishment; it is God himself holding his hand and pressing it rather hard. For, if he remains constant, what he will discover buried deep under the sound of his own lamentations is the pearl of the silence of God.

THE NECESSARY AND THE GOOD

These selections taken from Weil's notebooks highlight her concept of "necessity," which is a crucial but difficult concept in Weil's thinking. It at once refers to the impersonal reign of cause and effect in the material world. As such it is distant from goodness. But it is also created by God, and obedient to God. As such it is not only a witness to God, but in our acceptance of it, as Christ's in affliction, becomes the focus of our consent to God's will. Thus while not the good, for those who read it properly, it is a vital link to the good.

The distance separating the necessary from the good. It needs to be contemplated incessantly. (NB 363)

God has entrusted all phenomena, without any exception, to the mechanism of this world. (NB 361)

The contradictions which the mind is brought up against form the only realities, the only means of judging what is real. There is no contradiction in what is imaginary. Contradiction is the test on the part of necessity. (NB 329)

Necessity is the veil of God.

Superposed readings: we should read necessity behind sensation, order behind necessity, and God behind order. (NB 266–67)

Providence: the best definition is in *Timaeus:* the good cause has persuaded the necessary cause.... Composition on two planes. But in a sense necessity limits good. In another sense not, for it is good that there should be necessity. (NB 254)

•

If one believes that God created in order to be loved, and that he cannot create anything which is God, and further that he cannot be loved by anything which is not God, he is then brought up against a contradiction. The contradiction contains in itself Necessity. On the other hand every contradiction resolves itself through the process of becoming. God has created a finite being, which says "I," which is unable to love God. Through the action of grace the "I" little by little disappears, and God loves himself by way of the creature, which empties itself, and becomes nothing. When it has disappeared... he goes on creating more creatures and helping them to de-create themselves.

Time arises out of the state of becoming implied by this contradiction.

The contradiction contained in this contradiction represents the whole of Necessity in a nutshell. (NB 330–31)

God's powerlessness. Christ was crucified; his Father let him be crucified; two aspects of the same powerlessness. God does not exercise his all-powerfulness; if he did so, we should not exist, nor would anything else. Creation: God chaining himself down by necessity — One may hope that the chains will fall at death; but one also ceases to exist as a separate being — Why is creation a good, seeing that it is inseparably bound up with evil? In what sense is it a good that I should exist, and not God alone? How should God love himself through the wretched medium of myself? — that I cannot understand. But everything that I suffer, God suffers it too, for that is the effect produced by necessity, the free play of which he refrains from violating. (For that reason was he man and is he matter, food.) (NB 191)

Relentless necessity, misery, distress, the crushing burden of poverty and of exhausting labor, cruelty, torture, violent death, constraint, terror, disease — all this is but the divine love. It is God who out of love withdraws from us so that we can love him. For if we were exposed to the direct radiance of his love, without the protection of space, of time, and of matter, we should be evaporated like water in the sun; there would not be enough "I" in us to make it possible to love, to surrender the "I" for love's sake. Necessity is the screen placed between God and us so that we can *be*. It is for us to pierce through the screen so that we cease to *be*. We shall never pierce through it if we do not understand that God lies beyond at an infinite distance, and that good lies in God alone. (NB 402)

God does not send sufferings and woes as ordeals; he lets Necessity distribute them in accordance with its own proper mechanism. Otherwise he would not be withdrawn from creation, as he has to be in order that we may *be* and can thus consent not to be any longer. The occasional contacts resulting from inspiration between his creatures and Him are less marvelous than is his everlasting absence, and constitute a less marvelous proof of his love.

God's absence is the most marvelous testimony of perfect love, and that's why pure necessity, the necessity which is manifestly so different from good, is so beautiful. (NB 403)

•

Without necessity, it is impossible to conceive the divine alone, or grasp it or participate in it in any other way. (NB 66)

"What a difference lies between the essence of the necessary and that of the good."

When we understand that, we are detached with respect to the good.

God and creation are One; God and creation are infinitely distant from each other: this fundamental contradiction is reflected in that between the necessary and the good. To feel this distance means a spiritual quartering, it means crucifixion. . . .

This distance can only be bridged by a descending movement, not by an ascending one. In the fact that God is able to bridge it lies the proof that he is the Creator. (NB 400)

The world is God's language to us. The universe is the Word of God, the Verbum. (NB 480)

Let us imagine two prisoners, in neighboring cells, who communicate by means of taps on the wall. The wall is what separates them, but it is also what enables them to communicate. It is the same with us and God. Every separation represents a bond. (NB 497)

Man is like a castaway, clinging to a spar and tossed by the waves. He has no control over the movement imposed on him by the water. From the highest heaven God throws him a rope. The man either grasps it or not. If he does, he is still subject to the pressures imposed by the sea, but these pressures are combined with the new mechanical factor of the rope, so that the mechanical relations between the man and the sea have changed. His hands bleed from the pressure of the rope, and he is sometimes so buffeted by the sea that he lets go, and then catches it again.

But if he voluntarily pushes it away, God withdraws it. (FLN 82)

SOME THOUGHTS
ON THE LOVE OF GOD

To believe in God is not a decision that we can make. All we can do is to decide not to give our love to false gods. In the first place, we can decide not to believe that the future contains for us an all-sufficient good. The future is made of the same stuff as the present. We are well aware that the good which we possess at present, in the form of wealth, power, consideration, friends, the love of those we love, the well-being of those we love, and so on, is not sufficient: yet we believe that on the day when we get a little more we shall be satisfied. We believe this because we lie to ourselves. If we really reflect for a moment we know it is false. Or again, if we are suffering illness, poverty, or misfortune, we think we shall be satisfied on the day when it ceases. But there too, we know it is false; so soon as one has got used to not suffering one wants something else. In the second place, we can decide not to confuse the necessary with the good. There are a number of things which we believe to be necessary for our life. We are often wrong, because we should survive if we lost them. But even if we are right, even if they are things whose loss might kill us or at least destroy our vital energy, that does not make them good; because no one is satisfied for long with purely and simply living. One always wants something more; one wants something to live for. But it is only necessary to be honest with oneself to realize that there is nothing in this world to live for. We have only to imagine all our desires satisfied; after a time we should become discontented. We should want something else and we should be miserable through not knowing what to want.

A thing that everyone can do is to keep his attention fixed upon this truth.

Revolutionaries, for example, if they didn't lie to themselves, would know that the achievement of the revolution would make them unhappy, because they would lose their reason for living. And it is the same with all desires.

Life as it is given to men is unbearable without recourse to lying. Those who refuse to lie and who prefer to realize that life is unbearable, though without rebelling against fate, receive in the end, from somewhere beyond time, something which makes it possible to accept life as it is.

Everyone feels the existence of evil and feels horror at it and wants to get free from it. Evil is neither suffering nor sin; it is both at the same time, it is something common to them both. For they are linked together; sin makes us suffer and suffering makes us evil, and this indissoluble complex of suffering and sin is the evil in which we are submerged against our will, and to our horror.

A part of the evil that is within us we project into the objects of our attention and desire; and they reflect it back to us, as if the evil came from them. It is for this reason that any place where we find ourselves submerged in evil inspires us with hatred and disgust. It seems to us that the place itself is imprisoning us in evil. Thus an invalid comes to hate his room and the people around him, even if they are dear to him; and workers sometimes hate their factory, and so on.

But if through attention and love we project a part of our evil upon something perfectly pure, it cannot be defiled by it; it remains pure and does not reflect the evil back on us; and so we are delivered from the evil.

We are finite beings, and the evil in us is also finite; therefore by this method, if human life lasted long enough, we could be absolutely sure of being delivered in the end, in this world itself, from all evil.

The words of the Lord's Prayer are perfectly pure. Anyone who repeats the Lord's Prayer with no other intention than to bring to bear upon the words themselves the fullest attention of which he is capable is absolutely certain of being delivered in this way from a part, however small, of the evil he harbors within him. It is the same if one contemplates the Blessed Sacrament with no other thought except that Christ is there; and so on.

Nothing is pure in this world except sacred objects and sacred texts, and the beauty of nature when looked at for itself and not as a background for day-dreams, and also, to a lesser degree, those human beings in whom God dwells and those works of art which are of divine inspiration.

That which is perfectly pure can be nothing other than God present in this world. If it were something other than God it would not be pure. If God were not present we could never be saved. In the soul in which this contact with purity has taken place, all its horror at the evil it harbors is changed into love for the divine purity. It was in this way that Mary Magdalene and the good thief became privileged by love.

The sole obstacle to the transmutation of horror into love is the self-regard which makes it painful to expose one's defilement to contact with purity. This can only be overcome if one has a kind of indifference about one's own defilement, so that one is capable of rejoicing, without regard to oneself, at the thought that something pure exists.

Contact with purity effects a transformation in evil. Only in this way can there be release from the indissoluble complex of suffering and sin. Through this contact, suffering gradually ceases to be mixed with sin; while sin transforms itself into simple suffering. This supernatural operation is called repentance. It is as though some joy were to shine upon the evil in us.

That there should have been one perfectly pure being present on earth was enough to make him the divine lamb which takes away the world's sin and to cause the greatest possible amount of the evil diffused around him to concentrate upon him in the form of suffering.

He has left some perfectly pure things as remembrances of himself; that is to say, things in which he is present, for otherwise their purity would fade away through being in contact with evil.

But people are not in churches all the time, and it is particularly desirable that this supernatural operation of transferring the evil from within oneself to outside should be able to occur in the places where everyday life is lived, and especially in places of work.

This can only be done through symbols making it possible to read the divine truth in the circumstances of daily life and work in the same way that they are expressed in phrases by written letters. For this purpose the symbols must not be arbitrary but must be found inscribed, by a providential arrangement, in the very nature of things. The Gospel parables are an example of this symbolism.

There is indeed an analogy between the divine truths and the mechanical relations which constitute the order of the world of sense. The law of gravity which is sovereign on earth over all material motion is the image of the carnal attachment which governs the tendencies of the soul. The only power that can overcome

gravity is solar energy. It is because this energy comes down to
earth and is received by plants that they are able to grow vertically upwards. It enters into animals and men through the act
of eating, and it is only thanks to this that we are able to hold
ourselves erect and lift things up. Every source of mechanical
energy — water power, coal, and very probably petroleum — de-
rives in the same way from it; so it is the sun that drives our
motors and lifts our airplanes, as it also lifts the birds. We cannot go and fetch this solar energy; we can only receive it. The
energy comes down. It enters into plants and is with the seed,
buried underground in darkness; it is there that its fertility becomes most active, inciting the movement from below upwards
which makes the wheat or the tree grow. Even in a dead tree or
a wooden beam it is still there, maintaining the vertical line; and
we use it to build houses. It is the image of grace, which comes
down to be buried in the darkness of our evil souls and is the
only source of energy which can counteract the trend towards
evil which is the moral law of gravity.

It is not the farmer's job to go in search of solar energy or even
to make use of it, but to arrange everything in such a way that
the plants capable of using it and transmitting it to us will receive
it in the best possible conditions. And the effort he puts into this
work does not come from himself but from the energy supplied to
him by food, in other words, by this same solar energy contained
in plants and in the flesh of animals nourished by plants. In the
same way, the only effort we can make towards the good is so to
dispose our soul that it can receive grace, and it is grace which
supplies the energy needed for this effort.

A farmer or husbandman is like an actor continually playing
a role in a sacred drama which represents the relations between
God and the creation.

It is not only the source of solar energy that is inaccessible to
man, but also the power which transforms this energy into food.
Modern science considers this power to reside in the vegetable
substance called chlorophyll; antiquity said sap instead of chlorophyll, but it comes to the same thing. Just as the sun is the image
of God, so the vegetable sap — which can use the solar energy,

and which makes plants and trees rise up straight in defiance of gravity, and which offers itself to be crushed and destroyed inside us and so to maintain our life — is the image of the Son, the Mediator. The farmer's whole work consists in serving this image.

Poetry like this should suffuse agricultural labor with a light of eternity. Without it, the work is so monotonous that the workers may easily sink into despairing apathy or seek the grossest relaxations; for their work reveals too obviously the futility which afflicts all human conditions. A man works himself to exhaustion in order to eat, and he eats in order to get strength to work, and after a year of labor everything is exactly as it was at the beginning. He works in a circle. Monotony is only bearable for man if it is lit up by the divine. But for this very reason a monotonous life is much the more propitious for salvation.

SOME REFLECTIONS
ON THE LOVE OF GOD

The love that God bears us is, at any moment, the material and substance of our very being. God's creative love, which maintains us in existence, is not merely a superabundance of generosity; it is also renunciation and sacrifice. Not only the Passion but the Creation itself is a renunciation and sacrifice on the part of God. The Passion is simply its consummation. God already voids himself of his divinity by the Creation. He takes the form of a slave, submits to necessity, abases himself. His love maintains in existence, in a free and autonomous existence, beings other than himself, beings other than the good, mediocre beings. Through love, he abandons them to affliction and sin. For if he did not abandon them they would not exist. His presence would annul their existence as a flame kills a butterfly.

Religion teaches that God created finite begins of different degrees of mediocrity. We human beings are aware that we are at the extreme limit, the limit beyond which it is no longer possible to conceive or to love God. Below us there are only the animals. We are as mediocre and as far from God as it is possible for creatures endowed with reason to be. This is a great privilege. It is for us, if he wants to come to us, that God has to make the longest journey. When he has possessed and won and transformed our hearts it is we in our turn who have to make the longest journey in order to go to him. The love is in proportion to the distance.

It was by an inconceivable love that God created beings so distant from himself. It is by an inconceivable love that he comes down so far as to reach them. It is by an inconceivable love that they then ascend so far as to reach him. It is the same love. They can only ascend by the same love which God bestowed on them when he came down to seek them. And this is the same love by which he created them at such a great distance from him. The Passion is not separable from the Creation. The Creation itself is a kind of passion. My very existence is like a laceration of God, a laceration which is love. The more mediocre I am, the more obvious is the immensity of the love which maintains me in existence.

The evil which we see everywhere in the world in the form of affliction and crime is a sign of the distance between us and God. But this distance is love and therefore it should be loved. This does not mean loving evil, but loving God through the evil. When a child in his play breaks something valuable, his mother does not love the breakage. But if later on her son goes far away or dies she thinks of the incident with infinite tenderness because she now sees it only as one of the signs of her child's existence. It is this way that we ought to love God through everything good and everything evil, without distinction. If we love only through what is good, then it is not God we are loving but something earthly to which we give that name. We must not try to reduce evil to good by seeking compensations or justifications for evil. We must love God through the evil that occurs, solely because everything that actually occurs is real and behind all reality stands God. Some realities are more or less transparent; others are completely opaque; but God is behind all of them, without distinction. It is for us simply to keep our eyes turned towards the point where he is, whether we can see him or not. If there were no transparent realities we should have no idea of God. But if all realities were transparent it would not be God but simply the sensation of light that we would be loving. It is when we do not see God, it is when his reality is not sensibly perceptible to any part of our soul, that we have to become really detached from the self in order to love him. That is what it is to love God.

For this it is necessary to keep one's eyes constantly turned towards God, without ever moving. Otherwise, how should we know the right direction when the opaque screen comes between the light and us? We have to remain absolutely motionless.

To remain motionless does not mean to abstain from action. It is spiritual, not material immobility. But one must not act, or, indeed, abstain from acting, by one's own will. In the first place, we must perform only those acts to which we are constrained by a strict obligation, and then those which we honestly believe to have been enjoined upon us by God; and finally, if there remains an indefinite zone, those to which a natural inclination prompts us, provided they involve nothing illegitimate. In the sphere of action, it is only the fulfillment of strict obligations that calls for an effort. And, as for acts of obedience to God, they are performed passively; whatever pains may accompany them, they call for no effort, strictly speaking; it is not active effort but rather patience and capacity to endure and suffer. Their model is the crucifixion of Christ. Even though an act of obedience, when seen from outside, may seem accompanied by a great expenditure of activity, there is in reality, within the soul, nothing but passive endurance.

There is, however, one effort to be made, and by far the hardest of all, but it is not in the sphere of action. It is keeping one's gaze directed towards God, bringing it back when it has wandered, and fixing it sometimes with all the intensity of which one is capable. This is very hard, because all the mediocre part of ourselves, which is almost the whole of us — which *is* us, and is what we mean when we say "I" — feels that this fixed gaze towards God condemns it to death. And it does not want to die. It rebels. It fabricates every falsehood that can possibly divert our attention.

One of these falsehoods is the false gods which are given the name of God. We may believe we are thinking about God when what we really love is certain people who have talked to us about him, or a certain social atmosphere, or certain ways of living, or a certain calm of soul, a certain source of joyful feeling, hope, comfort, or consolation. In such cases the mediocre part of the soul is perfectly safe; even prayer is no threat to it.

Another falsehood has to do with pleasure and pain. We are well aware that the lure of pleasure or the fear of pain sometimes makes us act, or fail to act, in ways which oblige us to turn our eyes away from God; and when this happens we think we have been conquered by pleasure or pain, but this is very often an illusion. Very often the pleasure or pain of the senses is simply a pretext employed by the mediocre part of us for turning away from God. In themselves they have not so much power; not even an intoxicating pleasure or a violent pain is so very difficult to renounce or endure. We see it done every day by very mediocre people. But it is infinitely difficult to renounce even a very slight pleasure or to expose oneself to a very slight pain solely for the sake of God, the true God, that is to say, the one who is in heaven and not anywhere else. Because to make that effort is an approach, not towards suffering but towards death; and towards a death which is more radical than that of the body and equally repellent to nature: the death of the thing within us that says "I."

It does sometimes happen that the flesh turns us away from God, but often when we think this has happened it is really the other way round. The soul being unable to bear the deadly presence of God, that searing flame, takes refuge behind the flesh and uses it like a screen. In this case it is not the flesh which makes us forget God; it is the soul which tries to forget God by burying itself within the flesh. This is no longer a question of weakness but of treason, and we are always tempted to this treason so long as the mediocre part of the soul is much stronger than the part that is pure. A fault very slight in itself may be an act of treason of this kind, and in that case it is infinitely worse than faults which are very bad in themselves but which are the result of weakness. Treason is not avoided by an effort, by doing violence to oneself, but by a simple act of choice. It suffices to regard as a stranger and enemy the part of us that wants to hide itself from God —

even if that part is almost the whole of us, even if it *is* us. We must constantly renew within ourselves the vow of adherence to that part of us which calls for God, even when it is still only infinitely small. This infinitesimal part, so long as we adhere to it, increases exponentially by a geometrical progression like the series 2, 4, 8, 16, 32, etc., as a seed grows, and this happens without our taking any part in the process. We can arrest this growth by refusing it our adherence, and we can retard it by failing to use our will against the unruly movements of the physical part of the soul. But nevertheless when it does take place this growth takes place in us without any action by us.

Another pitfall, another deception by the mediocre part of us in its attempts to avoid death, is the misplaced effort towards the good, or towards God. This is a particularly dangerous deception because it is very difficult to understand why such efforts are false. Everything seems to suggest that the mediocre part of us is much better informed than we are about the conditions of salvation, so that one is impelled to believe in the existence of something like the devil. There are people whose manner of seeking God is like a man making leaps into the air in the hope that, if he jumps a little higher each time, he will end by staying up there and rising into heaven. This is a vain hope. In Grimm's tale of "The Valiant Little Tailor" there is a trial of strength between the little tailor and a giant. The giant hurls a stone high into the air, so that it takes a very, very long time to fall down again. The little tailor, who has a bird in his pocket, says he can do much better and that the stones he throws don't come down; and he releases his bird. Everything without wings always comes down to earth again. People who make athletic leaps towards heaven are too absorbed in the muscular effort to be able to look up to heaven; and in this matter the looking up is the one thing that counts. It is what makes God come down. And when God has come down to us he raises us, he gives us wings. The only effective and legitimate use of our muscular efforts is to keep at bay and suppress whatever may prevent us from looking up; they are negatively useful. The part of the soul which is capable of looking at God is surrounded by barking, biting, destructive dogs.

They must be controlled by the whip. But there is also no objection to employing lumps of sugar when it is possible. In any case, whether by the whip or by sugar — both are in fact needed, in different proportions for different temperaments — what matters is to train the dogs and compel them to silence and immobility. This training is one of the conditions for spiritual ascension but it is not itself an elevating force. God alone is the elevating power, and he comes when we look towards him. To look towards him means to love him. There is no other relation between man and God except love. But our love for God should be like a woman's love for a man, which does not express itself by making advances but consists only in waiting. God is the Bridegroom, and it is for the bridegroom to come to the one he has chosen and speak to her and lead her away. The bride-to-be should only wait.

Pascal's words "Thou wouldst not seek me if thou hadst not found me" are not the true expression of the relations between man and God. Plato is much more profound when he says: "Turn away with your whole soul from the things which pass." It is not for man to seek, or even to believe in God. He has only to refuse his love to everything which is not God. This refusal does not presuppose any belief. It is enough to recognize, what is obvious to any mind, that all the goods of this world, past, present, or future, real or imaginary, are finite and limited and radically incapable of satisfying the desire which burns perpetually within us for an infinite and perfect good. All men know this, and more than once in their lives they recognize it for a moment, but then they immediately begin deceiving themselves again so as not to know it any longer, because they feel that if they knew it they could not go on living. And their feeling is true, for that knowledge kills, but it inflicts a death which leads to a resurrection. But they do not know that beforehand; all they foresee is death; they must either choose truth and death or falsehood and life. If one makes the first choice and holds to it, if one persists indefinitely in refusing to devote the whole of one's love to things unworthy of it, which means everything in this world without exception, that is enough. It is not a matter of self-questioning or searching. A man has only to persist in this refusal, and one day or another

God will come to him. He will see and hear and cling to God, as Electra to Orestes; he will possess the certainty of an irrecusable reality. This does not mean that he will become incapable of doubting; to doubt is always both a faculty and a duty of the human mind; but if doubt presents itself one has only to entertain it unreservedly of what is uncertain and confirms the certainty of what is certain. For any man of whom God has taken possession the doubt concerning the reality of God is purely abstract and verbal, much more abstract and verbal than the doubt concerning the reality of the things of sense. When such a doubt presents itself one has only to entertain it unreservedly to discover how abstract and verbal it is. Consequently, the problem of faith does not arise. Until God has taken possession of him, no human being can have faith, but only simple belief; and it hardly matters whether or not he has such a belief because he will arrive at faith equally well through incredulity. The only choice before man is whether he will or will not attach his love to this world. Let him refuse to attach it, let him stay motionless, without searching, waiting in immobility and without even trying to know what he awaits, and it is absolutely certain that God will come all the way to him. To search is to impede rather than to facilitate God's operation. The man of whom God has taken possession no longer searches at all in the sense in which Pascal seems to use the word "search."

How could we search for God, since he is above, in a dimension not open to us? We can only advance horizontally; and if we advance in this way, seeking our good, and the search succeeds, this result will be illusory and what we have found will not be God. A little child who suddenly perceives that he has lost his mother in the street runs about, crying, in all directions; but he is wrong. If he had the sense and courage to stay where he is and wait, she would find him sooner. We must only wait and call out. Not call upon someone, while we still do not know if there *is* anyone; but cry out that we are hungry and want bread. Whether we cry for a long time or a short time, in the end we shall be fed, and then we shall not believe but we shall *know* that there really is bread. What surer proof could one ask for than to have eaten it? But before one has eaten, it is neither needful nor particularly useful to believe in bread. What is essential is to know that one is hungry; and this is not belief, it is absolutely certain knowledge which can only be obscured by lies. All those who believe that food exists, or will one day be produced, in this world, are lying.

The food of heaven not only makes the good grow in us but it destroys the evil, which our own efforts can never do. The quantity of evil in us can be reduced only by fixing our gaze upon something perfectly pure.

FURTHER REFLECTIONS ON THE LOVE OF GOD

These selections are meant to underline the concept of "de-creation" of the self in Weil's thinking. As should be apparent from them, as well as in her understanding of prayer, this "de-creation" is simultaneous to a re-creation of a new self in God.

Desire and De-creation

An experimental ontological proof. I have not the principle of rising in me. I cannot climb to heaven through the air. It is only by directing my thoughts towards something better than myself that I am drawn upwards by this something. If I am really drawn up, this something which draws me is real. No imaginary perfection can draw me upwards even by a fraction of an inch. For an imaginary perfection is mathematically at the same level as I am who imagine it — neither higher nor lower. What draws one up is directing one's thoughts towards a veritable perfection. (NB 434)

The love of self is the only love; but only God can love himself. That is why there is no other love open to us than to pray that God may love himself through us. (NB 193)

We possess only what we renounce. What we don't renounce escapes us. In this sense, we can possess nothing whatever without passing through God. (NB 544–45)

God created me as a non-being which has the appearance of existing, in order that through love I should renounce this apparent existence and be annihilated by the plenitude of being. (FLN 96)

Destruction is the opposite extreme of de-creation. One must try to conceive this clearly....

Redemptive suffering. When a human being is in a state of perfection; when by the help of grace he has completely destroyed the "I" in himself; if then he falls to the point of affliction that by nature corresponds for him, always supposing the "I" in him to be intact, to the destruction of the "I" from without — that represents for him the plenitude of the Cross. Affliction can no longer destroy the "I" in him; for the "I" no longer exists in him, having entirely disappeared and made room for God. But affliction produces an effect on the plane of perfection equivalent to the destruction of the "I" from without. It produces the absence of God. "My God, my God, why hast thou forsaken me?"

If the soul that falls into this affliction has partly abolished the "I" in itself in order to make room for God, but not completely so, the affliction produces the double effect; both the destruction of the "I" from without and the absence of God; expiatory suffering and redemptive suffering. But it is only in the state of perfection that, if one may so express it, the fullness of the absence of God can take place.

The purely external destruction of the "I" is quasi-infernal suffering. The external destruction with which the soul associates itself through love is expiatory suffering. The bringing about of God's absence is redemptive suffering. (NB 342)

•

To be for Christ just what this pencil is for me, when, with my eyes closed, I feel its point in contact with the table. It lies within our power to be mediators between God and that part of creation which has been entrusted to us. Our consent is necessary in order that through the medium of ourselves God may be able to perceive his own creation. With our consent he is able to perform this marvel. It would only be necessary for me to manage to withdraw myself from my own soul for this table that is in front of me to have the incomparable good fortune of being seen by God. God can only love in us this consent we show in withdrawing in order to allow him to pass, in the same way as he himself, the Creator, has withdrawn in order to allow us to *be*. There is no other meaning but love attached to this double operation, just as a father gives his child the wherewithal to enable the child to give his father a present on his birthday. God, who is nothing else but Love, has not created anything but Love. (NB 401)

Prayer

Example of prayer.
  Say to God:
  Father, in the name of Christ, grant me this.
  That I may be unable to will any bodily movement, or even any attempt at movement, like a total paralytic. That I may be incapable of receiving any sensation, like someone who is completely blind, deaf, and deprived of all the senses. That I may be unable to make the slightest connection between two thoughts, even the simplest, like one of those total idiots who not only cannot count or read but have never learned to speak. That I may be insensible to every kind of grief and joy, and incapable of any love for any being or thing, and not even for myself, like old people in the last stage of decrepitude.
  Father, in the name of Christ, grant me all this in reality.
  May this body move or be still, with perfect suppleness or rigidity, in continuous conformity to thy will. May my faculties of hearing, sight, taste, smell, and touch register the perfectly accurate impress of thy creation. May this mind, in fullest lucidity, connect all ideas in perfect conformity with thy truth. May this sensibility experience, in their greatest possible intensity and in all their purity, all the nuances of grief and joy. May this love be an absolutely devouring flame of love of God for God. May all this be stripped away from me, devoured by God, transformed into Christ's substance, and given for food to afflicted me whose

body and soul lack every kind of nourishment. And let me be a paralytic — blind, deaf, witless, and utterly decrepit.

Father, effect this transformation now, in the name of Christ; and although I ask it with imperfect faith, grant this request as if it were made with perfect faith.

Father, since thou art the Good and I am mediocrity, rend this body and soul away from me to make them into things for your use, and let nothing remain of me, forever, except this rending itself, or else nothingness.

Words like this are not efficacious unless they are dictated by the Spirit. One does not voluntarily ask for such things. One comes to it in spite of oneself. In spite of oneself, yet one comes to it. One does not consent to it with abandon, but with a violence exerted upon the entire soul by the entire soul. But the consent is total and unreserved, and given by a single movement of the whole being. (FLN 244–45)

•

In relation to God, we are like a thief who has burgled the house of a kindly householder and been allowed to keep some gold. From the point of view of the lawful owner this gold is a gift; from the point of view of the burglar it is a theft. He must go and give it back. It is the same with our existence. We have stolen a little of God's being to make it ours. God has made a gift of it. But we have stolen it. We must return it.

The soul which has attained to seeing the light must lend its vision to God and turn it on the world.

The self, as it disappears, must become an empty space through which God and the creation contemplate each other.

Then the part of the soul that has seen God must transform every relation with a created being or thing into a relation between that being and God.

Every relation between two or several created things — whether thinking beings or matter — is one of God's thoughts. We ought to desire a revelation of the thought of God corresponding to each relation with our fellow men or with the material objects with which we are involved.

To refrain from conceiving those relations for ourselves is only a step on the way. The end is to conceive each of them, specifically, as a thought of God's. (FLN 269)

•

First half of the Lord's Prayer.

"Hallowed be thy name."

By using the name of God we can orient our attention towards the true God, who is beyond our reach and is inconceivable by us. Without the gift of this name we should have only a false earthly God, conceivable by us. This name alone makes it possible for us to have a Father in the Heavens, about which we know nothing.

"Thy kingdom come."

Having absolutely relinquished every kind of existence, I accept existence, of no matter what kind, solely though conformity to God's will.

"On earth as it is in heaven."

I accept the eternal decree of the divine Wisdom and its entire unfolding in the order of time.

It is not easy to think all those things with all one's soul. To do so, we have great need of the supersubstantial bread, of forgiveness for our past trespasses, and of deliverance from evil. (FLN 361)

2

Reflections on Love and Faith

Attention, taken to its highest degree, is the same thing as prayer. It presupposes faith and love. (NB 205)

Waiting patiently in expectation is the foundation of the spiritual life. (FLN 99)

REFLECTIONS ON THE RIGHT USE OF SCHOOL STUDIES WITH A VIEW TO THE LOVE OF GOD

This little essay was prepared for students at a Catholic girls' school at Father Perrin's request. In its wonderfully clear presentation, it contains the key to the very important notion of "attention" in Weil. "Attention"—the suspension of one's own self as a center of the world and a making oneself available to the reality of another being, is the key both to prayer and, in later works, to justice in Weil. Its paradigm is the self-emptying of Christ on the Cross.

The key to a Christian conception of studies is the realization that prayer consists of attention. It is the orientation of all the attention of which the soul is capable towards God. The quality of the attention counts for much in the quality of the prayer. Warmth of heart cannot make up for it.

The highest part of the attention only makes contact with God when prayer is intense and pure enough for such a contact to be established; but the whole attention is turned towards God.

Of course school exercises only develop a lower kind of attention. Nevertheless, they are extremely effective in increasing the power of attention that will be available at the time of prayer, on condition that they are carried out with a view to this purpose and this purpose alone.

Although people seem to be unaware of it today, the development of the faculty of attention forms the real object and almost the sole interest of studies. Most school tasks have a certain intrinsic interest as well, but such an interest is secondary. All tasks that really call upon the power of attention are interesting for the same reason and to an almost equal degree.

School children and students who love God should never say: "For my part I like mathematics"; "I like French"; "I like Greek." They should learn to like all these subjects, because of them develop that faculty of attention which, directed towards God, is the very substance of prayer.

If we have no aptitude or natural taste for geometry, this does not mean that our faculty for attention will not be developed by wrestling with a problem or studying a theorem. On the contrary it is almost an advantage.

It does not even matter much whether we succeed in finding the solution or understanding the proof, although it is important to try really hard to do so. Never in any case whatever is a genuine effort of the attention wasted. It always has its effect on the spiritual plane and in consequence on the lower one of the intelligence, for all spiritual light lightens the mind.

If we concentrate our attention on trying to solve a problem of geometry, and if at the end of an hour we are no nearer to doing so than at the beginning, we have nevertheless been making progress each minute of that hour in another more mysterious dimension. Without our knowing or feeling it, this apparently barren effort has brought more light into the soul. The result will one day be discovered in prayer. Moreover, it may very likely be felt in some department of the intelligence in no way connected with mathematics. Perhaps he who made the unsuccessful effort will one day be able to grasp the beauty of a line of Racine more vividly on account of it. But it is certain that this effort will bear its fruit in prayer. There is no doubt whatever about that.

Certainties of this kind are experimental. But if we do not believe in them before experiencing them, if at least we do not behave as though we believed in them, we shall never have the experience that leads to such certainties. There is a kind of contradiction here. Above a given level this is the case with all useful knowledge concerning spiritual progress. If we do not regulate our conduct by it before having proved it, if we do not hold on to it for a long time by faith alone, a faith at first stormy and without light, we shall never transform it into certainty. Faith is the indispensable condition.

The best support for faith is the guarantee that if we ask our Father for bread, he does not give us a stone. Quite apart from explicit religious belief, every time that a human being succeeds in making an effort of attention with the sole idea of increasing his grasp of truth, he acquires a greater aptitude for grasping it, even if his effort produces no visible fruit. An Eskimo story explains the origin of light as follows: "In the eternal darkness, the crow, unable to find any food, longed for light, and the earth was illumined." If there is a real desire, if the thing desired is really light, the desire for light produces it. There is a real desire when there is an effort of attention. It is really light that is desired if all other incentives are absent. Even if our efforts of attention seem for years to be producing no result, one day a light that is in exact proportion to them will flood the soul. Every effort adds a little gold to a treasure no power on earth can take away. The useless efforts made by the Curé d'Ars, for long and painful years, in his attempt to learn Latin bore fruit in the marvelous discernment that enabled him to see the very soul of his penitents behind their words and even their silences.

Students must therefore work without any wish to gain good marks, to pass examinations, to win school successes; without any reference to their natural abilities and tastes; applying themselves equally to all their tasks, with the idea that each one will help to form in them the habit of that attention which is the substance of prayer. When we set out to do a piece of work, it is necessary to wish to do it correctly, because such a wish is indispensable in any true effort. Underlying this immediate objective, however, our deep purpose should aim solely at increasing the power of attention with a view to prayer; as, when we write, we draw the shape of the letter on paper, not with a view to the shape, but with a view to the idea we want to express. To make this the sole and exclusive purpose of our studies is the first condition to be observed if we are to put them to the right use.

The second condition is to take great pains to examine squarely and to contemplate attentively and slowly each school task in which we have failed, seeing how unpleasing and second-rate it is, without seeking any excuse or overlooking any mistake or any of our tutor's corrections, trying to get down to the origin of each fault. There is a great temptation to do the opposite, to give a sideways glance at the corrected exercise if it is bad and to hide it forthwith. Most of us do this nearly always. We have to withstand this temptation. Incidentally, moreover, nothing is more necessary for academic success, because, despite all our efforts, we work without making much progress when we refuse to give our attention to the faults we have made and our tutor's corrections.

Above all it is thus that we can acquire the virtue of humility, and that is a far more precious treasure than all academic progress. From this point of view it is perhaps even more useful to contemplate our stupidity than our sin. Consciousness of sin gives us the feeling that we are evil, and a kind of pride sometimes finds a place in it. When we force ourselves to fix the gaze, not only of our eyes but of our souls, upon a school exercise in which we have failed through sheer stupidity, a sense of our mediocrity is borne in upon us with irresistible evidence. No knowledge is more to be desired. If we can arrive at knowing this truth with all our souls we shall be well established on the right foundation.

If these two conditions are perfectly carried out there is no doubt that school studies are quite as good a road to sanctity as any other.

To carry out the second, it is enough to wish to do so. This is not the case with the first. In order really to pay attention, it is necessary to know how to set about it.

Most often attention is confused with a kind of muscular effort. If one says to one's pupils: "Now you must pay attention," one sees them contracting their brows, holding their breath, stiffening their muscles. If after two minutes they are asked what they have been paying attention to, they cannot reply. They have been concentrating on nothing. They have not been paying attention. They have been contracting their muscles.

We often expend this kind of muscular effort on our studies. As it ends by making us tired, we have the impression that we have been working. That is an illusion. Tiredness has nothing to do with work. Work itself is the useful effort, whether it is tiring or not. This kind of muscular effort in work is entirely barren, even if it is made with the best of intentions. Good intentions in such cases are among those that pave the way to hell. Studies conducted in such a way can sometimes succeed academically from the point of view of gaining marks and passing examinations, but that is in spite of the effort and thanks to natural gifts; moreover such studies are never of any use.

Will power, the kind that, if need be, makes us set our teeth and endure suffering, is the principal weapon of the apprentice engaged in manual work. But, contrary to the usual belief, it has practically no place in study. The intelligence can only be led by desire. For there to be desire, there must be pleasure and joy in the work. The intelligence grows and bears fruit only in joy. The joy of learning is as indispensable in study as breathing is in running. Where it is lacking there are no real students, but only poor caricatures of apprentices who, at the end of their apprenticeship, will not even have a trade.

It is the part played by joy in our studies that makes of them a preparation for spiritual life, for desire directed towards God is the only power capable of raising the soul. Or rather, it is God alone who comes down and possesses the soul, but desire alone draws God down. He comes only to those who ask him to come; and he cannot refuse to come to those who implore him long, often, and ardently.

Attention is an effort, the greatest of all efforts perhaps, but it is a negative effort. Of itself, it does not involve tiredness. When we become tired, attention is scarcely possible any more, unless we have already had a good deal of practice. It is better to stop working altogether, to seek some relaxation, and then a little later to return to the task; we have to press on and loosen up alternately, just as we breathe in and out.

Twenty minutes of concentrated, untired attention is infinitely better than three hours of the kind of frowning application that leads us to say with a sense of duty done: "I have worked well!"

But, in spite of all appearances, it is also far more difficult. Something in our soul has a far more violent repugnance for true attention than the flesh has for bodily fatigue. This something is much more closely connected with evil than is the flesh. That is why every time that we really concentrate our attention, we destroy the evil in ourselves. If we concentrate with this intention, a quarter of an hour of attention is better than a great many good works.

Attention consists of suspending our thought, leaving it detached, empty, and ready to be penetrated by the object; it means holding in our minds, within reach of this thought, but on a lower level and not in contact with it, the diverse knowledge we have acquired which we are forced to make use of. Our thought should be in relation to all particular and already formulated thoughts, as a man on a mountain who, as he looks forward, sees also below him, without actually looking at them, a great many forests and plains. Above all our thought should be empty, waiting, not seeking anything, but ready to receive in its naked truth the object that is to penetrate it.

All wrong translations, all absurdities in geometry problems, all clumsiness of style, and all faulty connection of ideas in compositions and essays, all such things are due to the fact that thought has seized upon some idea too hastily, and being thus prematurely blocked, is not open to the truth. The cause is always that we have wanted to be too active; we have wanted to carry out a search. This can be proved every time, for every fault, if we trace it to its root. There is no better exercise than such a tracing down of our faults, for this truth is one to be believed only when we have experienced it hundreds and thousands of times. This is the way with all essential truths.

We do not obtain the most precious gifts by going in search of them but by waiting for them. Man cannot discover them by his own powers, and if he sets out to seek for them he will find in their place counterfeits of which he will be unable to discern the falsity.

The solution of a geometry problem does not in itself constitute a precious gift, but the same law applies to it because it is the image of something precious. Being a little fragment of particular truth, it is a pure image of the unique, eternal, and living Truth, the very Truth that once in a human voice declared: "I am the Truth."

Every school exercise, thought of in this way, is like a sacrament.

In every school exercise there is a special way of waiting upon truth, setting our hearts upon it, yet not allowing ourselves to go out in search of it. There is a way of giving our attention to the data of a problem in geometry without trying to find the solution or to the words of a Latin or Greek text without trying to arrive at the meaning, a way of waiting, when we are writing, for the right word to come of itself at the end of our pen, while we merely reject all inadequate words.

Our first duty towards school children and students is to make known this method to them, not only in a general way but in the particular form that bears on each exercise. It is not only the duty of those who teach them but also of their spiritual guides. Moreover the latter should bring out in a brilliantly clear light the correspondence between the attitude of the intelligence in each one of these exercises and the position of the soul, which, with its lamp well filled with oil, awaits the Bridegroom's coming with confidence and desire. May each loving adolescent, as he works at his Latin prose, hope through this prose to come a little nearer to the instant when he will really be the slave — faithfully waiting while the master is absent, watching and listening — ready to open the door to him as soon as he knocks. The master will then make his slave sit down and himself serve him with meat.

Only this waiting, this attention, can move the master to treat his slave with such amazing tenderness. When the slave has worn himself out in the fields, his master says on his return, "Prepare my meal, and wait upon me." And he considers the servant who only does what he is told to do to be unprofitable. To be sure in the realm of action we have to do all that is demanded of us, no matter what effort, weariness, and suffering it may cost, for he who disobeys does not love; but after that we are only unprofitable servants. Such service is a condition of love, but it is not enough. What forces the master to make himself the slave of his slave, and to love him, has nothing to do with all that. Still less is it the result of a search the servant might have been bold enough to undertake on his own initiative. It is only watching, waiting, attention.

Happy then are those who pass their adolescence and youth in developing this power of attention. No doubt they are no nearer to goodness than their brothers working in fields and factories. They are near in a different way. Peasants and workmen possess a nearness to God of incomparable savor which is found in the depths of poverty, in the absence of social consideration, and in the endurance of long, drawn-out sufferings. If, however, we consider the occupations in themselves, studies are nearer to God because of the attention which is their soul. Whoever goes through years of study without developing this attention within himself has lost a great treasure.

Not only does the love of God have attention for its substance; the love of our neighbor, which we know to be the same love, is made of this same substance. Those who are unhappy have no need for anything in this world but people capable of giving them their attention. The capacity to give one's attention to a sufferer is a very rare and difficult thing; it is almost a miracle; it *is* a miracle. Nearly all those who think they have this capacity do not possess it. Warmth of heart, impulsiveness, pity are not enough.

In the first legend of the Grail, it is said that the Grail (the miraculous vessel that satisfies all hunger by virtue of the consecrated Host) belongs to the first comer who asks the guardian of the vessel, a king three-quarters paralyzed by the most painful wound, "What are you going through?"

The love of our neighbor in all its fullness simply means being able to say to him: "What are you going through?" It is a recognition that the sufferer exists, not only as a unit in a collection or a specimen from the social category labeled "unfortunate," but as a man, exactly like us, who was one day stamped with a special mark by affliction. For this reason it is enough, but it is indispensable, to know how to look at him in a certain way.

This way of looking is first of all attentive. The soul empties itself of all its own contents in order to receive into itself the being it is looking at, just as he is, in all his truth.

Only he who is capable of attention can do this.

So it comes about that, paradoxical as it may seem, a Latin prose or a geometry problem, even though they are done wrong, may be of great service one day, provided we devote the right kind of effort to them. Should the occasion arise, they can one day make us better able to give someone in affliction exactly the help required to save him, at the supreme moment of his need.

For an adolescent, capable of grasping this truth and generous enough to desire this fruit above all others, studies could have their fullest spiritual effect, quite apart from any particular religious belief.

Academic work is one of those fields containing a pearl so precious that it is worthwhile to sell all our possessions, keeping nothing for ourselves, in order to be able to acquire it.

THEORY OF THE SACRAMENTS

This text was written in 1943 while Weil was in London. It was sent to Maurice Schumann, who was her great good friend dating from their days at the École Normale Supérieure. High up in the Free French administration, he had been instrumental in getting Weil to London to work for the Free French and was

one of a few who knew well her religious thinking while she
was alive.

Human nature is so arranged that a desire of the soul, unless it
passes through the flesh by means of actions, movements, and
postures that naturally correspond to it, hasn't any reality for the
soul. It dwells there only as a phantom. It doesn't act on the soul.

On this arrangement is founded the possibility of a certain self-
control by means of the will through a natural link between the
will and the muscles.

But if the exercise of the will can, on the one hand, to a limited degree prevent the soul from falling into evil, on the other
hand, it cannot by itself increase the proportion of good to evil
in the soul.

If one does not have as much money as he would like in his
wallet, he has to go to a bank to get it. He is not going to find it
on his own person, since he lacks it.

The good we do not have in ourselves we cannot procure for
ourselves, no matter what effort of the will we make. We can
only receive it.

We receive it infallibly on one condition. That condition is
desire. But not the desire of a partial good.

Desire directed towards the pure, perfect, total, absolute good
alone can put a little more good into the soul than it had before.
When a soul desires like this, its progress is proportional to the
intensity of the desire and its duration.

But only real desires act on the soul. The desire for absolute
good is effective inasmuch — and only inasmuch — as it is real.

But if the movements and postures of the body can have for
their objects only things here below, how can this desire find
passage into reality through the flesh?

It is impossible.

Wherever it is certain that something indispensable for salvation is impossible, it is certain that there really exists a supernatural possibility.

For all that concerns the absolute good and contact with it,
the proof by perfection (sometimes falsely called the ontological

proof) is not only sound, but the only sound proof. It follows immediately from the concept of the good itself. The proof by perfection is to the good as necessity is to demonstration in geometry.

In order that the desire for absolute good should pass through the flesh, it is necessary that some object here below be able to put, by some sign and covenant, the flesh into relation to the absolute good.

While there might be a relation between the absolute good and the flesh, that is not to say that it is a good for the flesh. It is the absolute good for the spirit that is in relation to the flesh.

A covenant concerning things here below can be concluded and ratified by humans, or between one person and himself.

A covenant concerning the absolute good can only be ratified by God.

(This idea of divine ratification is, in the canon of the Mass, what immediately precedes the consecration.)

A divine ratification necessarily implies a direct revelation of God, and perhaps even necessarily implies the Incarnation.

The only things which can be signs of God are those which God has established as such.

By a covenant established by God between God and human beings, a piece of bread signifies the person of Christ. Since by virtue of the fact that a covenant ratified by God is infinitely more real than nature, its reality as bread, while remaining, becomes simple appearance relative to the infinitely more real reality that constitutes its significance.

In covenants established between human beings, the original nature of the thing that symbolizes the covenant is more real than its symbolic nature. In a covenant established by God, it is the opposite. But the divine signifying that supervenes over nature does so in an infinitely greater degree of reality than nature does over human signifying.

If one believes that the contact with the piece of bread is a contact with God, in this case, in the contact with the bread, the desire for contact with God, which was only an inclination, passes the test of reality.

By this same fact, and because in this domain desiring is the unique condition for receiving, there is a real contact between the soul and God.

In things here below, credulity produces illusion. It is only with respect to divine things and at the moment when a soul has its desire and attention turned towards God that believing has the virtue of producing the real, and that by the effect of desire. The believing that is productive of reality is called faith.

Grace is at once that which is both the most exterior thing to us and the most interior. The good comes to us only from outside, but it penetrates us only as the good to which we consent. Consent is only real at the moment when the flesh makes it real by an act.

We cannot transform ourselves; we can only be transformed. But we can be transformed only if we want good. A bit of matter hasn't the power to transform us. But if we believe that it has that ability by God's willing it so, and that for this reason we should eat it, we really accomplish an act of welcome towards the wished-for transformation, and by this fact transformation descends upon the soul from the heights of heaven. By that, the bit of matter has the supposed virtue.

The sacrament is an arrangement which corresponds in an irreproachable, perfect manner to the double character of grace, both as something submitted to and consented to, and as involving the relation of human thought with the flesh.

There is a double condition in the supernatural mechanism of the sacrament for belief to be able to have this power.

It is necessary that the object of desire not be anything other than the unique, pure, perfect, total, absolute good which is inconceivable for us. Many people use the word "God" as an honorific title for conceptions that their own souls have made up or which have been furnished by the surrounding milieu. There are plenty of conceptions of this type, which more or less resemble the true God, but which the soul can think without having in fact oriented its attention outside this world. In this case, though, however it may appear to be occupied by God, the soul continues to sojourn in this world, and belief, according to the law of this world, is a maker of illusions, not of truth.

This state, however, is not without hope, for the names of God and Christ have by themselves a sort of power that can over time draw the soul out of this state and into truth.

The second condition is that the belief in a certain identity between the piece of bread and God should have penetrated one's entire being to the point of impregnating, not the intelligence which cannot have any part therein, but all the rest of the soul — imagination, sensibility, even the flesh itself.

When these two conditions exist, and when the approach of the contact with the bread is to the point of submitting desire to the test of reality, something really happens in the soul.

Insofar as a desire does not have contact with the real, its existence does not produce conflict within the soul. For example, if a man sincerely desires to expose himself to death as a soldier in the service of his country, and if it is not possible to take one step towards bringing that about, say, if he were half paralyzed, his desire would never come into conflict with the fear of death.

If a man has the possibility either of going into battle or not, then if he decides to go, if he takes steps to do so, if he succeeds, if he is under fire, if he is sent on an extremely perilous mission, if he is killed, then it is quite certain that at some moment of this unfolding of duty the fear of death will arise in his soul and be fought. The moment can be situated at any point of this process according to temperament and the nature of his imagination. It is only at the approach of this moment, though, that desire, exposed to death, becomes real.

It is the same with desire for contact with God. Insofar as it is not yet real, it remains dormant in the soul.

But when the conditions for a true sacrament exist and the sacrament is about to take place, the soul is divided.

One part of the soul, which can at the moment be imperceptible to consciousness, aspires to the sacrament; it is the part of truth in the soul, for "whosoever does the truth goes to the light."

But all of the mediocre part of the soul is repulsed by the sacrament, hating it and fearing it more than the flesh of an animal which recoils to avert impending death. For "whosoever does mediocre things hates the light."

Thus begins a separation between the good seed and the tares. Christ said: "I did not come to bring peace, but a sword." And St. Paul says: "The word of God is living and active, sharper than any two-edged sword, piercing until it divides soul from spirit, joints from marrow, and discerns the feelings and thoughts of the heart" (Heb. 4:12).

Communion is then a passage through fire which burns and destroys a part of the soul's impurities. The following communion destroys still another part. The amount of evil contained in any human soul is finite; the divine fire is inexhaustible.Thus at the end of this mechanism, despite our faults and falterings, as long as there has been no betrayal and deliberate refusal of the good, or where death has not come accidentally before the end, the passage into the state of perfection is infallible.

The more real that the desire for God is, and the more real that the contact with God is through the sacrament, the more violent is upheaval of the mediocre part of the soul; an upheaval comparable to the jerking away of living flesh that is at the point of being thrust into the fire. According to the particular case, this upheaval has principally the color of repulsion, or of hatred or of fear.

When the soul is in a state where the approach to the sacrament is more painful than the march towards death, it is nearly at the threshold beyond which martyrdom is easy.

In its desperate effort to survive and to escape the fire's destruction, the mediocre part of the soul, with a fevered activity, invents arguments. It is indifferent to the arsenal from which it takes them, including theology and all its warnings about unworthy participation in the sacraments.

On the condition that these thoughts are absolutely not listened to by the soul in which they arise, this interior tumult is infinitely blessed.

The more violent this interior movement of recoil, revolt, and fear is, the more certain it is that the sacrament will destroy a great deal of evil in the soul and transport it closer to perfection.

"The mustard seed is the smallest of the seeds."

The imperceptible atom of pure good lodged in the soul by

a movement of real desire towards God is this seed. If it is not uprooted by a willing treason, it will infallibly give out branches in time where the birds of heaven will roost.

Christ said: "The kingdom of God is as if someone would scatter seed on the ground, and would sleep and rise night and day, and the seed would sprout and grow, he does not know how. The earth produces of itself, first the stalk, then the head, then the full grain in the head. But when the grain is ripe, at once he goes in with his sickle, because the harvest has come" (Mark 4:26).

When the soul has once crossed the threshold by a real contact with the pure good — the interior tumult before the sacrament is perhaps a certain sign of this — there is nothing left to do but remain in immobile waiting.

Motionless waiting is not the absence of external activity. External activity, insofar as it is rigorously imposed by human obligations or by particular commandments of God, is a part of this immobility of the soul; doing less or more both equally upset the posture of motionless waiting.

An activity exactly congruent to that which is commanded is a condition of the soul's waiting, as, with a child who is studying, sitting still is a condition of paying attention.

But as physical immobility is something other than attention, is not effective by itself, so it is with prescribed acts for the soul which has reached this state.

In the same way as the truly attentive person has no need to impose immobility on himself in order to pay attention, but, on the contrary, as soon as his thought fixes itself on a problem it automatically suspends the movements which would disturb it, in the same way prescribed acts unfold automatically from a soul in a state of motionless waiting.

Insofar as perfection is distant, these acts are frequently mixed with pain, sadness, fatigue, an appearance of interior struggle, and grave failings; yet, insofar as there is not any willed treason in the soul, there is something irresistible in their accomplishment.

One cannot dispense with these prescribed acts, but it is not because of them that he is open to being loved by God.

"Who among you would say to your slave who has just come in from plowing or tending sheep in the field, 'Come here at once and take your dinner?' Will you not say, 'Prepare my dinner, and gird yourself and serve me till I eat and drink and afterward you shall eat and drink?' Does he thank the servant because he did what was commanded? So you also, when you have done all that is commanded you, say, 'We are unworthy servants; we have only done what was commanded of us' " (Luke 17:7).

The slave who receives love, gratitude, and even service from his master is not the one who plows and harvests. That is somebody else.

Not that there is any question of two ways of serving God. These two slaves represent the same soul under two different relations, or, moreover, two inseparable parts of the soul.

The slave who will be loved is the one who remains motionless before the door, watching, waiting, attentive, wanting to open it when he hears a knock.

Neither fatigue, nor hunger, nor solicitations, nor friendly invitations, nor injuries, blows, or jests from his comrades, nor rumors that circulate around him that his master is dead or that the master is irritated with him and resolved to do him evil, none of these things will distract him in the slightest from his motionless waiting.

"Be like those who are waiting for their master to return from the wedding banquet, so that they may open the door for him when he comes and knocks. Blessed are those slaves who the master finds alert when he comes; truly I tell you, he will fasten his belt and have them sit down to eat, and he will come and serve them."

The state of waiting thus fulfilled is what is ordinarily called patience.

But the Greek word *hupomené* is infinitely more beautiful and charged with a different significance.

It indicates one who waits without budging, despite all the bodily blows rained on him to make him budge.

Karpophorousin en hupomené.

"They will bear fruit in patient endurance" (Luke 8:15).

THREE THEOLOGICAL CONCEPTS

These selections on "the supernatural," "mystery," and "faith" give some sense of Weil's insightful contributions to some very important conceptions for theology and the philosophy of religion. The "supernatural" is not something just "out there"; it is what engages us in active religious faith. Its reality in the world of necessity is the transformation of us. That gives us radically different ways that we need to think and talk of God and of human faith, and of the relation between faith and reason. Faith is neither given by reason, nor defies it. It shapes how we think.

The Supernatural

To think on God, to love God, is nothing else than a certain way of thinking on the world. (NB 25)

The object of my search is not the supernatural, but this world. The supernatural is the light. We must not presume to make an object of it, or else we degrade it. (NB 173)

Postulate. In the sphere of the intelligence, the supernatural is that which is dark and a source of light. Since the greater cannot come out of the less in the order of value (*postulate requiring to be examined*), this darkness is more luminous than what, for our intelligence, is luminous. We are continually moving from a lesser to a greater amount of light; when we jump, passing through some darkness, something has pulled us. Descending light.

To ask oneself first of all: Is the notion of the supernatural indispensable? And next: Where and in what circumstances is it indispensable to resort to it?

If it is indispensable, it is so in order to ponder the human condition (and not simply the history of the Jewish people in the first place, and then that of Europe).

The Word is the light which comes with every man. (NB 226)

•

The soul's attitude towards God is not a thing that can be verified, even by the soul itself, because God is elsewhere, in heaven, in secret. If one thinks to have verified it, there is really some earthly thing masquerading under the label of God. One can verify only whether the behavior of the soul bears the mark of an experience of God.

In the same way, a bride's friends do not go into the nuptial chamber; but when she is seen to be pregnant they know that she has lost her virginity.

There is no fire in a cooked dish, but one knows that it has been on the fire.

On the other hand, even though one may think to have seen the flames under them, if the potatoes are raw it is certain they have not been on the fire.

It is not the way a man talks about God, but the way he talks about the things of this world that best shows whether his soul has passed through the fire of the love of God. In this matter no deception is possible. There are false imitations of the love of God, but not of the transformation it effects in the soul, because one has no idea of this transformation except by passing through it oneself.

In the same way, the proof that a child can do division is not that he can recite the rule, but that he can divide. If he recites the rule, I don't know whether he understands it. If I give him some difficult sums in division and he gets the answers right, I have no need to make him explain the rule. It doesn't even matter if he is incapable of it, or doesn't know the name of the operation. I know that he understands it. If the child who could repeat the rule adds the numbers up instead of dividing them, I know he doesn't understand it.

In the same way, I know the author of the *Iliad* knew and loved God and the author of the Book of Joshua did not.

When a man's way of behaving towards things and men, or simply his way of regarding them, reveals supernatural virtues, one knows that his soul is no longer virgin; it has slept with God, perhaps even without knowing it, like a girl violated in her sleep. That has no importance; it is only the fact that matters....

A painter does not draw the spot where he is standing. But in looking at his picture I can deduce his position by relation to the things drawn.

On the other hand if he puts himself into the picture I know for certain that the place where he shows himself is not the place where he is.

According to the conception of human life expressed in the acts and words of a man I know (I mean I would know if I possessed discernment) whether he sees life from a point in this world or from above in heaven.

On the other hand, when he talks about God I cannot discern (and yet sometimes I can . . .) whether he is speaking from within or externally. . . .

The Gospel contains a conception of human life, not a theology.

If I turn on an electric light at night out of doors I don't judge its power by looking at the bulb, but by seeing how many objects it lights up.

The brightness of a source of light is appreciated by the illumination it projects upon non-luminous objects.

The value of a religious or, more generally, a spiritual way of life is appreciated by the amount of illumination thrown upon the things of this world.

Earthly things are the criterion of spiritual things.

This is what we generally don't want to recognize, because we are frightened of a criterion.

The virtue of anything is manifested outside the thing. . . .

If a man gives bread to a beggar in a certain way or speaks in a certain way about a defeated army, I know that his thought has been outside this world and sat with Christ alongside the Father who is in heaven. (FLN 145–48)

•

The body is always a balance for motives, a perpetual balance, perpetually in motion. What we call "I," "me" is only a motive.

But the supernatural lies in this, that for a moment the balance stops moving and remains in suspension. After the stoppage, the same forces act upon it, only now it is more exact. (NB 97)

Mystery

When, while the attention is being (or after it has been) fixed on unintelligible mysteries, truths appear that are absolutely clear and simple for the intelligence, but which the latter had not hitherto perceived, this constitutes a criterion. (NB 576)

•

The notion of mystery is legitimate when the most logical and most rigorous use of the intelligence leads to an impasse, to a contradiction which is inescapable in this sense: that the suppression of one term makes the other term meaningless and that to pose one term necessarily involves posing the other. Then, like a lever, the notion of mystery carries thought beyond the impasse, to the other side of the unopenable door, beyond the domain of intelligence and above it. But to arrive beyond the domain of the intelligence one must have traveled all through it, to the end, and by a path traced with unimpeachable rigor. Otherwise one is not beyond it but on this side of it....

Another criterion is that when the mind has nourished itself with mystery, by a long and loving contemplation, it finds that by suppressing and denying the mystery it is at the same time depriving the intelligence of treasures which are comprehensible to it, which dwell in its domain and which belong to it.

The intelligence cannot control mystery itself, but it possesses perfectly the power of control over the roads leading to mystery, those that mount up and those that lead down again from it. Therefore it can recognize, while remaining absolutely loyal to itself, the existence within the soul of a faculty which is superior to itself and which conducts thought on to a higher plane than its own. This faculty is supernatural love.

The consented subordination of all the natural faculties of the soul to supernatural love is faith. (FLN 131)

•

There are three mysteries, three incomprehensible things, in this world: beauty, justice, and truth.

They are the three things recognized by all men as standards for everything in the world. The incomprehensible is the standard for the known. (FLN 292)

The Nature of Faith

There are two sorts of atheism, one of which is a purification of the notion of God. ...

Perhaps everything which is evil has another aspect, which is a purification in the course of progress towards good, and a third one which is the higher good. ... Three aspects to be carefully distinguished, for it is very dangerous for thought and for the effective conduct of life to confuse them. ...

Good which is defined in the way in which one defines evil should be rejected. Evil does reject it. But the way it rejects it is a bad one.

[Cases of true contradictories: God exists; God doesn't exist. Where lies the problem? No uncertainty whatsoever. I am absolutely certain that there is a God, in the sense that I am absolutely certain that my love is not illusory. I am absolutely certain that there is not a God, in the sense that I am absolutely certain that there is nothing real which bears a resemblance to what I am able to conceive when I pronounce that name, since I am unable to conceive God — But that thing, which I am able to conceive is not an illusion — This impossibility is more immediately present to me than is the feeling of my own personal existence.] (NB 126–27)

To read God in every manifestation, without exception, but according to the true manifestation relationship proper to each appearance. To know in what way each appearance is not God.

Faith, a gift of reading...

Faith. To believe that nothing of what we are able to grasp is God. Negative faith. But also, to believe that what we are unable to grasp is more real than what we are able to grasp; that our power to grasp is not the criterion of reality, but on the contrary is deceptive. To believe, finally, that what lies beyond our grasp appears nevertheless — hidden. (NB 220)

•

Religion insofar as it is a source of consolation is a hindrance to true faith; and in this sense atheism is a purification. I have to be an atheist with that part of myself which is not made for God. Among those in whom the supernatural part of themselves has not been awakened, the atheists are right and the believers wrong.

The mysteries of the Catholic faith — and those of other religious or metaphysical traditions — are not designed in order to be believed by all parts of the soul. The presence of Christ in the host is not a fact in the same way that the presence of my friend Paul in Paul's body is a fact; otherwise it would not be supernatural. (Both facts are, moreover, equally incomprehensible — but not in the same way.) The Eucharist should not then be an object of belief for the part of me which apprehends facts. That is where Protestantism is true (or, with respect to the Incarnation, where Deism is true). But this presence of Christ in the host is not a symbol either, for a symbol is the combination of an abstraction and an image; it is something which human intelligence can represent to itself; it is not supernatural. There the Catholics are right, not the Protestants. Only that part of myself which is made for the supernatural should adhere to these mysteries. But this adherence is more a matter of love than of belief. What is, then, the distinction between love and faith?

The role of the intelligence — that part of us which affirms and denies, formulates opinions — is solely one of submission. All that I conceive of as true is less true than these things of which I cannot conceive the truth, but which I love. That is why St. John of the Cross calls faith a night. With those who have received a Christian education, the lower parts of the soul become attached to these mysteries when they have no right at all to do so. That is why such people need a purification of which St. John of the Cross describes the stages. Atheism and incredulity constitute an equivalent of such a purification.

We should not seize upon these mysteries as truths, for that is impossible, but recognize the subordination to these mysteries which we love of all that we seize upon as truths. The intelligence can recognize this subordination by feeling that the love of these mysteries is the source of conceptions which it can seize upon as truths. Such would seem to be the relationship between faith and love.

In the sphere of the relationship between man and the supernatural we must seek a more than mathematical precision, something even more precise than science. Such is also one of the uses to which science should be put.

The mysteries of faith cannot be either affirmed or denied; they must be placed above that which we affirm or deny. (NB 238–39)

•

Faith. It is for the intelligence to discern what forms the object of supernatural love. For it must perfectly discern all that which is at the level of intelligible truth and all that which is below it. All that which is neither the one nor the other is the object of supernatural love. Discrimination on the part of the intelligence is essential in order to separate supernatural love from attachment. For we can be attached to something which we name God.

Love is a disposition of the supernatural part of the soul. Faith is a disposition of *all* the parts of the soul — and of the body as well — each one assuming with regard to the object of love the attitude suitable to its nature. Justice, according to Plato. (In the Scriptures, too, faith, is continually assimilated to justice.) (NB 241)

•

The real aim is not to see God in all things; it is that God through us should see the things that we see. God has got to be on the side of the subject and not on that of the object during all those intervals of time when, forsaking the contemplation of the light, we imitate the descending movement of God so as to turn ourselves towards the world. (NB 358)

•

Link between truth and obedience. Certainty is the obedience of the intelligence (and certainly not submission to an external authority, even one that is accepted by faith). (FLN 81)

•

Belief is aroused by the beauty of the texts and by the light one gains upon the human condition through meditating on them. (FLN 123)

•

Faith is not a contact with God; otherwise it would not be called a night and a veil. It is the submission of those parts which have no contact with God to the one which has. (FLN 132)

To believe that the desire for good is always fulfilled — that is faith, and whoever has it is not an atheist.

To believe in a God who can leave in darkness those who desire light, and reciprocally, that is not to have faith.

Faith is the certainty of a domain other than this inextricable mixture of good and evil which constitutes this world, a domain in which good only produces good and evil only produces evil. (FLN 137–38)

•

If a man truly believes that the rite will really bring about his re-generation, the fact of asking for it implies doing such violence to the evil within him that all the other circumstances accompanying his request are insignificant by comparison. To kneel in the snow for three days and nights would add nothing to the difficulty. To condemn to death the evil within oneself is so difficult as to be at the extreme limit of possibility. Nothing can be more difficult.

But to make a request of this kind only reaches the extreme limit of difficulty if one is certain that the rite one is asking for will involve the death of the evil within oneself.

That is why faith is an indispensable intermediary for making the body an arbiter in the spiritual conflict of the soul with itself.

Faith creates the truth to which it adheres. The certainty that a rite or ceremony gives spiritual regeneration confers that efficacy on it; and this is not the effect of a phenomenon of suggestion, which would imply illusion and falsehood, but of the mechanism here analyzed.

The domain of faith is the domain of truths created by certainty. It is in this domain that faith is legitimate and is a virtue. A virtue creative of truth.

It is necessary to discriminate this domain. (FLN 291)

•

That God is the good is a certainty. It is a definition. And it is even certain that God — in some way that I do not know — is reality. This is certain, and not a matter of faith. But it is an object of faith that every thought of mine which is a desire for good brings me nearer to the good. It is only by experience that I can test this. And even after the experience it is still not an object of proof but only of faith.

To possess the good consists in desiring the good; therefore the relevant article of faith — which is the sole article of true faith — is concerned with fecundity, with the self-multiplying faculty of every desire for good.

From the mere fact that a part of the soul truly and purely and exclusively desires the good, it follows that at a later point in time a larger part of it will desire the good — unless it refuses to consent to this development.

To believe that is to possess faith. (FLN 307)

•

All I can do is to desire the good. But whereas all other desires are sometimes effective and sometimes not, according to circumstances, this one desire is always effective. The reason is that, whereas the desire for gold is not the same thing as gold, the desire for good is itself a good. (FLN 316)

3

Justice and Human Society

The most important part of teaching = to teach what it is to *know* (in the scientific sense). Nurses. (FLN 364)

Excepting some notebook selections, these essays and other se-lections all come from Weil's last writings in London, where she turned her attention again to social matters. The essays are par-ticularly important for understanding her most developed ideas on justice. The epigraph for this section is the last entry Weil made in her notebooks. "Nurses" refers to her project for a front-line nursing corps (see the introduction, p. 20).

REFLECTIONS ON CULTURE AND SOCIETY

These brief selections give some of Weil's crucial revisionings of the nature of culture and society in her last months in London. Most important is the idea of the metaxu. *The term is taken from the Greek and means "intermediary." Weil, who had al-ways worried about social pressure and the "herd instinct," uses it here to talk about how culture* positively *functions in spiritual life. All things of this world, all things of necessity, including human society, can have a sort of sacramental nature and can function as bridges to God, or ways in which God can be im-plicitly present in human life. As such, she saw it was vitally important to read social life as an intermediary; too often, she thought, we go about social life in quite the opposite way, as an end in itself. To read social relations in this way is key to understanding her last political and social writings in London.*

The Metaxu

What is it evil to destroy? Not that which is base, for that doesn't matter. Not that which is high, for, even should we want to, we cannot touch that. The *metaxu*. The *metaxu* form the region of good and evil.

If we create for ourselves *metaxu* in organic life itself, then we cannot lose them so long as we remain alive.

No man should be deprived of a single one of his *metaxu*. (NB 48)

•

Necessity in the things of the soul. Those who look for it are generally materialists, atheists (in the true sense of the word), which falsifies everything. What is necessity without labor? Necessity must be regarded as that which imposes conditions. (NB 217)

•

Metaxu. Every representation which draws us towards the non-representable. Need for *metaxu* in order to prevent us from seizing hold of nothingness instead of full being. (NB 233)

True earthly goods are *metaxu.* We can only respect those of others (e.g., foreign cities) if we regard those we possess ourselves as *metaxu* — which implies that one is on the way towards the point where one will be able to do without them. (NB 258)

The directing of the attention towards God needs to be sustained by intermediaries. This is so even in a church, to which one goes for the above purpose. How much more so, therefore, in the case of work.

These intermediaries must not be manufactured; they must be found inscribed in the nature of things, for they exist there providentially. (NB 596)

•

We should turn everything into an intermediary leading towards God (everything — occupations, events, public functions, etc.). This does not mean adding God on to everything (it is then the imaginary form of God). But each thing must be wrought upon to bring about a change so that it may be made transparent to the light.

Knowing an alphabet is not the same thing as knowing how to read. After having learned an alphabet, it is possible to spend the rest of one's life without being able to read a single word printed in that alphabet. (NB 328–29)

Culture

To be rooted is perhaps the most important and least recognized need of the human soul. It is one of the hardest to define. A human being has roots by virtue of his real, active, and natural participation in the life of a community which preserves in living shape certain particular treasures of the past and certain particular expectations for the future. This participation is a natural one, in the sense that it is automatically brought about by place, conditions of birth, profession, and social surroundings. Every human being needs to have multiple roots. It is necessary for him to draw well nigh the whole of his moral, intellectual, and spiritual life by way of the environment of which he forms a natural part. (NR 41)

Nothing can have as its destination anything other than its origin.

The contrary idea, the idea of progress, is poison. We are experiencing this. The root, which, mixed with faith, has produced this fruit ought to be torn up. (FLN 79)

Pure science is a contemplation of the order of the world as necessity.

Necessity appears only through the method of proof.

Obvious kinship between the idea of necessity and obedience....

Orient science towards obedience and not towards power. But

this *is* the orientation of pure science, which is contemplation of necessity. (FLN 79)

A life in which the supernatural truths would be read in every kind of work, in every act of labor, in all festivals, in all hierarchical social relations, in all art, in all science, in all philosophy.

Yes, but what about war? In war, one should read the supernatural truths concerning evil. (FLN 173)

Collective life reflects the beauty of the world in one part by orientation towards God, in another part by its association in time with the rhythm of the seasons. (EL 158–59)

Science is an effort to perceive the order of the universe. It follows that it is a contact of human thought with eternal wisdom. It is something like a sacrament.

In all the peoples of antiquity — except the Romans, of course — lived the thought that inert matter, by its submission to necessity, gives man the example of obedience to God.

This thought permits embracing in a single act of the mind science as the investigation of the beauty of the world, art as the imitation of the beauty of the world, justice as the equivalent of the beauty of the world in human affairs, and love towards God insofar as he is the author of the beauty of the world.

Thus is recovered a unity lost for centuries.

It is necessary to add work as "physical contact" with the beauty of the world through the pain of effort.

Not only is the submission of matter to necessity the image of our obedience, but this necessity is the image of the supernatural operation of grace. (EL 159–60)

What is culture?

The formation of the attention.

Participation in the spiritual and poetic treasures accumulated by humanity across the ages. Knowledge of man. Concrete knowledge of good and evil. (EL 160)

Work

Through work, man turns himself into matter, like Christ does through the Eucharist. Work is like death.

We must needs pass through death — that the old man may die. But death is not a suicide. We have got to be killed — to endure the gravitational force, the weight of the world. When the universe is weighing upon the back of a human being, is there anything surprising in the fact that it should hurt him? (NB 78–79)

Work and passion. By work every being subjects himself to matter, is pinned down by matter. Whether it be a question of suffering or not, it is at any rate one of submission. It means the abandonment of personal will — an abandonment which remains uncompensated.

In work, everything is an intermediary, everything is a means — the material, the tool, the body, and the soul.

Essential condition for any non-servile form of work. (NB 597)

A society in which the two poles are obedience and attention — labor and study. . . .

Labor is consent to the order of the universe. (FLN 358)

ARE WE STRUGGLING FOR JUSTICE?

This essay is crucial for spelling out what justice means for Weil. It is a matter of consent to the other, just as God's justice is found in seeking our consent for the creation.

"The examination of what is just is carried out only when there is equal necessity on each side. Where there is one who is strong and one who is weak, the possible is done by the first and accepted by the second."[1]

So speak in Thucydides the Athenians who have come to bring an ultimatum to the wretched little city of Melos.

They add: "Regarding the gods we have the belief, regarding men the certainty that by a necessity of nature each one always commands wherever he has the power to do so."[2]

---

1. Thucydides V, 89.
2. Ibid., V, 105.

They thus expressed in two sentences the whole of Realpolitik. Only the Greeks of this period could conceive evil with this marvelous lucidity. They no longer loved the good, but their fathers, who had loved it, had handed down its light to them. They made use of it to recognize the truth of evil. Men had not yet immersed themselves in lies. This is why it was not the Athenians but the Romans who founded an empire.

Those two sentences are the sort that shock kindly souls. But to the extent to which a man has not experienced their truth in his flesh, his blood and his entire soul, he cannot yet have access to the real love of justice.

The Greeks defined justice admirably as mutual consent.

"Love," says Plato, "neither does nor suffers injustice, neither among the gods nor among men. For whatever is done to Love it is not done by force, since force cannot lay hands on Love. And when he acts he does not act by force; for all consent to obey Love in everything. Where there is agreement by mutual consent there is justice, say the laws of the royal city."[3]

This makes the opposition of the just and the possible in the words cited by Thucydides very clear. When there is equal strength on both sides, one seeks the conditions for mutual consent. When someone does not have the capacity to refuse, one is not going to look for a way of obtaining his consent. Thus only those conditions which correspond to objective necessities are examined. The consent of matter is all that one seeks.

In other words, human action has no other rule or limit than obstacles. It has no contact with realities other than these. Matter imposes obstacles which are determined by its own mechanism. A man may impose obstacles through a power to refuse which he sometimes has and sometimes not. When he does not have it, he does not constitute an obstacle nor, consequently, a limit. In relation to the action and to the one who performs it, he has no existence.

Whenever there is action, thought moves towards its goal. Without obstacles the goal would be attained as soon as thought

---

3. Plato, *Symposium*.

of. Sometimes that is how it is. A child sees his mother from afar after an absence, and he is in her arms almost before knowing that he has seen her. But when immediate fulfillment is impossible, thought, at first focused on the goal, is inevitably claimed by the obstacles.

It is claimed by them alone. Where there are none, it does not stop. Anything not constituting an obstacle to the substance of its action — for example men without the capacity to refuse — is transparent to it as is completely clear glass to sight. It is not up to it to stop there anymore than it is up to sight to discern glass.

Someone who does not see a pane of glass does not know that he does not see it. Someone who, being placed differently, does see it, does not know that the other does not see it.

When our will finds expression outside ourselves in actions performed by others, we do not waste our time and our power of attention in examining whether they have consented to this. This is true for all of us. Our attention, given entirely to the success of the undertaking, is not claimed by them as long as they are docile.

That is necessary. If it were otherwise, things would not get done, and if things did not get done, we would perish.

But because of this, action is tainted by sacrilege. For human consent is a sacred thing. It is what man grants to God. It is what God comes in search of when like a beggar he approaches men.

What God unceasingly begs each man to grant is the very thing which other men despise.

Rape is a terrible caricature of love from which consent is absent. After rape, oppression is the second horror of human existence. It is a terrible caricature of obedience. Consent is as essential to obedience as it is to love.

The butchers of the city of Melos were pagan in the hateful sense of the word, whereas their fathers had not been so. In a single sentence they completely and perfectly defined the pagan conception. "Concerning the gods we believe that by a necessity of nature each one always commands wherever he has the power to do so."

The Christian faith is nothing but the cry affirming the contrary. The same is true of the ancient doctrines of China, India, Egypt, and Greece.

The act of creation is not an act of power. It is an abdication. Through this act a kingdom was established other than the kingdom of God. The reality of this world is constituted by the mechanism of matter and the autonomy of rational creatures. It is a kingdom from which God has withdrawn. God, having renounced being its king, can enter it only as a beggar.

As for the cause of this abdication, Plato expresses it thus: "He was good."[4]

The Christian doctrine contains the notion of a second abdication. " . . . Being in the state of God, He did not regard equality with God as a prize. He emptied himself. He assumed the state of slavery. . . . He humbled himself to the point of being made obedient even unto death. . . . Even though He was the Son, what He suffered taught Him obedience."[5]

These words could have been an answer to the Athenian murderers of Melos. They would have really made them laugh. And rightly so. They are absurd. They are mad.

But just as the content of these words is absurd and mad, so, proportionately, it would be absurd and mad for anyone at all to impose upon himself the necessity of seeking consent where there is no power of refusal. It is the same madness.

But Aeschylus said to Prometheus: "It is good to love to the point of seeming mad."

The madness of love, once it has seized a human being, completely transforms the modalities of action and thought. It is akin to the madness of God. The madness of God consists in needing man's free consent. Men made with love for their fellows suffer under the thought that everywhere in the world human beings serve as intermediaries to the will of others without having consented to it. They find it unbearable to know that this is often true of their own will and of that of the groups to which they belong. In all their actions and thoughts relating to human beings,

4. *Timaeus* 29e.
5. Philippians 2:6–9.

whatever be the nature of the relation, each man, without exception, appears to them as constituted by a faculty to consent freely to the good through love, a faculty imprisoned in the soul and in flesh. It is not doctrines, conceptions, inclinations, intentions, wants, which thus transform the mechanism of human thought. For this madness is needed.

A man with no money, gnawed by hunger, cannot see anything to do with food without suffering. For him, a town, a village, a street, is nothing but restaurants and grocery stores with vague houses all around. If, as he walks down the street, he comes across a restaurant, it is impossible for him not to stop for a while. And yet, it seems, there is no obstacle in his way here. But there is one for him, because of his hunger. Other passersby, strolling along aimlessly or going about their business, move through these streets as if past a theater set. For him, each restaurant, turned into an obstacle by this invisible mechanism, has the fullness of reality.

But the condition for this is that he be hungry. None of this occurs unless there is a need in him which gnaws his body.

Men struck by the madness of love need to see the faculty of free consent spreading throughout this world, in all forms of human life, for all human beings.

"What can it matter to them?" think reasonable men. But it is not their fault, the poor wretches. They are made so. Their stomach is upset. They hunger and thirst for justice.

Just as all restaurants are real for the starving wretch, so are all human beings for these men. For them alone. It is always a particular play of circumstances or a particular gift of personality which in normal people gives rise to the feeling that some particular human being really exists. These fools, they can direct their attention at any human being whatever, placed in any circumstances whatever, and receive from him the shock of reality.

But for this they must be made, they must carry within them a need as destructive of the natural equilibrium of the soul as is hunger of the functioning of the organs.

The great mass of people who lack the power to grant or

refuse consent do not, collectively, have the slightest chance of raising themselves to the possession of such a power without some complicity within the ranks of those in command. But there is no such complicity except among the mad. And the more madness there is below, the more chances there are that it will appear by contagion at the top.

To the extent to which at any given time there is some madness of love among men, to that extent there is some possibility of change in the direction of justice: and no further.

One must be blind to oppose justice to charity; to believe that they have a different scope, that one is wider than the other, that there is a charity beyond justice or a justice falling short of charity.

When the two notions are opposed, charity is no more than a whim, often of base origin, and justice is no more than social constraint. Those who do not realize this have either never been in one of those situations where there is every license for injustice, or else were so entrenched in falsehood as to believe that they had no difficulty in acting justly.

It is just not to steal from shop counters. It is charitable to give alms. But a shopkeeper can send me to prison. A beggar, even if his life depended on my succor, would not report me to the police if I refused him.

Many controversies between right and left are no more than a conflict between a preference for individual whim and a preference for social constraint; or, more accurately perhaps, between dread of social constraint and dread of individual whim. Neither charity nor justice has anything to do with this.

Justice has as its object the exercise of the faculty of consent on earth. To preserve it religiously wherever it exists, to try to create conditions for it where it is absent, that is to love justice.

The single, so beautiful, word "justice" comprises the entire significance of the three words of the French motto. Liberty is a real possibility of granting consent. Men do not need equality except in relation to it. The spirit of fraternity consists in desiring it for all.

Consent is made possible by a life containing motives for consenting. Destitution, privations of soul and body, prevent consent from being able to operate in the depths of the heart.

The expression of consent is not altogether indispensable. A thought which is not expressed is imperfect, but it is real, it can clear its own indirect paths towards expression. Expression which has no thought corresponding to it is a lie, and there is always, everywhere, the possibility of a lie.

Since obedience is in fact the imprescribable law of human life, the only distinction that needs to be made is between obedience which is consented to and obedience which is not. Where obedience is consented to there is freedom: there, and nowhere else.

It is not in parliament, nor in the press, nor in any institution that freedom can dwell. It dwells in obedience. Where obedience does not have everywhere a daily and permanent flavor of freedom, there is no freedom. Freedom is the flavor of true obedience.

The forms and the expressions of consent vary greatly in different traditions and milieux. Thus a society of men much freer than we are can, if it is very different from us, appear despotic to us in our ignorance. We do not realize that outside the realm of words there are differences of language and possibilities of misinterpretation. And we maintain this ignorance within us because it gratifies in us all a shameful, unacknowledged taste for conquests which enslave under the pretense of liberating.

On the other hand there is a certain kind of devotedness linked to slavery which, far from being a sign of consent, is the direct effect of a system of brutal constraint; for in affliction human nature desperately seeks compensations no matter where. Hatred, dull indifference, blind attachment, anything will do for it so long as it escapes the thought of affliction.

Where there is freedom there is a blossoming of happiness, beauty, and poetry; that, perhaps, is its only certain mark.

Democratic thought contains a serious error — it confuses consent with a certain form of consent, which is not the only one and which can easily, like any form, be mere form.

Our parliamentary democracy was hollow, for we despised the

leaders that we chose, we bore a grudge against those we did not choose, and we obeyed all of them unwillingly.

Consent is neither to be bought nor sold. Consequently, whatever the political institutions, in a society where monetary transactions dominate most of social life, where almost all obedience is bought and sold, there can be no freedom.

Just as oppression is analogous to rape, so the dominance of money over work, pushed to the point where money becomes the prime motive for work, is analogous to prostitution.

Enthusiasm is not consent: it is a superficial rapture of a soul. It is to consent what the infatuated attachment of a philanderer to a woman of easy virtue is to the union of marriage.

Where people know no motives other than constraint, money, and a carefully maintained and stimulated enthusiasm, there is no possibility of freedom.

That on the whole is the case today, in varying degrees, in all the countries of the white race, and in all those where the influence of the white race has penetrated.

If England is to quite a large extent an exception, that is because there is still a little of the past, living and intact in her. This past, present throughout the land, has at this time[6] been the only glimmer of salvation for the world. But there is no similar treasure elsewhere.

Freedom is unfortunately not something close at hand for us to recover, a familiar object snatched away by surprise. It is something to be created.

We, the French, have once launched into the world the principles of 1789. But we are wrong to take pride in this. For neither then nor since have we been able either to think them or to put them into practice. Remembering them should rather teach us humility.

It is true that humility seems a sacrilege where one's country is concerned. But this prohibition places a barrier between modern patriotism and the spirit of justice and love. The Pharisaic

---

6. The essay was written during the war.

spirit poisons at its source any sentiment from which humility is excluded.

Modern patriotism is a sentiment inherited from pagan Rome, one which, moreover, has come down to us across so many Christian centuries without having been baptized. For this very reason it is not in keeping with the spirit of 1789; the two cannot be reconciled in truth, as would be indispensable for the French.

Such as it is, it can steel some men to the point of supreme sacrifice, but it cannot nourish the desperate masses of today. They need something which would not be Corneillian, but would be familiar, human, warming, simple, and without pride.

For obedience to be consented to, one needs above all something to love, something for the love of which men consent to obey.

Something to love, not through hating its opposite, but in itself. The spirit of consenting obedience stems from love, not from hatred.

Hatred, it is true, provides an imitation at times very dazzling, but nevertheless mediocre, of poor quality, of little endurance, one which quickly spends itself.

Something to love not for its glory, its prestige, its glitter, its conquests, its radiance, its future prospects, but for itself, in its nakedness and its reality, as a mother whose son has come first in the entrance examinations to the École Polytechnique loves something else in him. Otherwise the feeling is not deep enough to be a permanent source of obedience.

What we need is something a people can love naturally from the depths of its heart, from the depths of its own past, out of its traditional aspirations, and not through suggestion, propaganda, or foreign import.

What we need is a love imbibed quite naturally with one's milk, a love which brings young people to conclude once and for all deep in the innermost part of their hearts a pact of fidelity of which a whole life of obedience is but an extension.

What we need is for the forms of social life to be so devised as to remind the people incessantly in the symbolic language most intelligible to it, most in harmony with its customs, traditions, and attachments, of the sacred character of this fidelity, the free consent from which it issues, the rigorous obligation arising from it.

From this point of view the Republic, universal suffrage, an independent trade union movement, are completely indispensable in France. But this is infinitely far from being sufficient, since these things had lost their significance for us and have only begun arousing interest again a long time after they had been destroyed.

As for the Empire, if the preceding suggestions contain any truth, they strictly oblige us on pain of lying to present all the problems concerning the colonies in a totally different light from hitherto.

We shall not find freedom, equality, and fraternity without a renewal of our forms of life, a creativity within the social fabric, an eruption of new inventions.

But we seem to be too exhausted for such an eruption.

Men as a whole have reached morally a degree of sickness at which there seems to be no cure other than a miraculous one. Miraculous means not impossible, but possible only in certain conditions.

The conditions in which a soul can be opened to grace are of a different kind from those of a mechanical operation. But they are determined even more rigorously. It is even more impossible to find some ruse, some trick which would permit their evasion.

It is not easy to fight for justice. It is not enough to discern which is the side of least injustice and, having joined it, to take up arms and expose oneself to the arms of the enemy. No doubt this is beautiful, more than words can say. But on the other side men do exactly the same.

What we need in addition is for the spirit of justice to dwell within us. The spirit of justice is nothing other than the supreme and perfect flower of the madness of love.

The madness of love turns compassion into a far more powerful motive for any kind of action, including fighting, than splendor, glory, or even honor.

It compels one to abandon everything for compassion and, as St. Paul says of Christ, to empty oneself.

Even amid unjustly inflicted suffering, it makes one consent to submit to the universal law by which every creature of this world is exposed to injustice. This consent preserves the soul from evil; in the soul where it is found, it has a miraculous power of transforming evil into good, injustice into justice; through it suffering, accepted with respect, without servility or rebelliousness, becomes something divine.

The madness of love draws one to discern and cherish equally, in all human milieux without exception, in all parts of the globe, the fragile earthly possibilities of beauty, of happiness, and of fulfillment; to want to preserve them all with an equally religious care; and where they are absent, to want to rekindle tenderly the smallest traces of those which have existed, the smallest seeds of those which can be born.

The madness of love imbues a part of the heart deeper than indignation and courage, the place from which indignation and courage draw their strength, with tender compassion for the enemy.

The madness of love does not seek to express itself. But it radiates irresistibly through accent, tone, and manner, through all thoughts, all words, and all actions, in all circumstances and without any exception. It makes impossible those thoughts, words, and actions through which it cannot radiate.

It truly is madness. It hurls one into risks one cannot run if one has given one's heart to anything at all that belongs to this world, be it a great cause, a Church, or a country.

The outcome to which the madness of love led Christ is, after all, no recommendation for it.

But we need not fear its perils. It does not dwell in us. If it did, it would be felt. We are reasonable people, as obviously befits those who concern themselves with the great matters of the world.

But if the order of the universe is a wise order, there must sometimes be moments when, from the point of view of earthly reason, only the madness of love is reasonable. Such moments can only be those when, as today, mankind has become mad from want of love.

Is it certain that today the madness of love may not be capable of providing the unhappy masses, hungry in body and soul, with a food far easier for them to digest than are inspirations from a less lofty source?

So then, being what we are, is it certain that we are at our post in the camp of justice?

DRAFT FOR A STATEMENT OF HUMAN OBLIGATIONS

There are three variants of this piece, of which this is the longest. It outlines many of the key themes of The Need for Roots. *The "profession of faith" is meant to be a sort of credo for those who will lead the government, and the shortest version of this piece is a condensation that could be spoken as such. How Weil intends this credo to work, as a sort of pole star, is given in this brief fragment:*

Sketch of the basis of a doctrine (especially for the use of study groups in France).

A doctrine is not sufficient, but it is indispensable to have one, in order to avoid being deceived by false doctrine. The sight of the polar star never tells the fisherman where he ought to go, but he will lose his direction in the night if he doesn't know how to recognize it.

Moreover, to conceive, comprehend, and adopt the best doctrine is easy. The fundamental truths are simple. The difficulty is in the application. More exactly, the difficulty is in being so nourished by it, of having so completely absorbed it, that application becomes instinctive.

But the first difficulty is the words. The truth is at the base of the heart of every man, but so profoundly hidden that it is difficult to translate it into language. Men have such a need of words that a thought which is not expressed in words can, by this fact, be impotent with respect to putting it into action. When we want something that

we cannot name, we can be made to believe that we want
something else, and derail the store of our energy towards
something mediocre or evil. (EL 151)

Profession of Faith

There is a reality outside the world, that is to say, outside space
and time, outside man's mental universe, outside any sphere
whatsoever that is accessible to human faculties. Corresponding
to this reality, at the center of the human heart, is the longing for
an absolute good, a longing which is always there and is never
appeased by any object in this world.

Another terrestrial manifestation of this reality lies in the absurd and insoluble contradictions which are always the terminus
of human thought when it moves exclusively in this world.

Just as the reality of this world is the sole foundation of facts,
so that other reality is the sole foundation of good.

That reality is the unique source of all the good that can exist
in this world: that is to say, all beauty, all truth, all justice, all
legitimacy, all order, and all human behavior that is mindful of
obligations.

Those minds whose attention and love are turned towards that
reality are the sole intermediary through which good can descend
from there and come among men.

Although it is beyond the reach of any human faculties, man
has the power of turning his attention and love towards it.

Nothing can ever justify the assumption that any man, whoever he may be, has been deprived of this power.

It is a power which is only real in this world insofar as it is
exercised. The sole condition for exercising it is consent.

This act of consent may be expressed, or it may not be, even
tacitly; it may not be clearly conscious, although it has really
taken place in the soul. Very often it is verbally expressed although it has not in fact taken place. But whether expressed
or not, the one condition suffices: that it shall in fact have
taken place.

If we are only saved by American money and machines we

shall fall back, one way or another, into a new servitude like the one which we now suffer. It must be remembered that Europe was not subjugated by invading hordes from another continent, or from Mars, who have only to be driven out again. She is wasted by an internal malady. She needs to be cured.

She cannot survive unless she is saved, at least in great measure, by her own exertions. Fortunately, she is not in a position to oppose the conqueror's idolatry with one of her own, because it is impossible for enslaved nations to be turned into idols. The conquered peoples can only oppose the conqueror with a religion.

If a faith were to arise in this unhappy continent, victory would be rapid, certain, and secure. That is obvious even on the strategic level. Our line of communication is the sea, and can be defended by submarines. Whereas the enemy's communications are on land, among the oppressed peoples, and they would be destroyed if all the land were set ablaze by a true faith.

But we cannot foster the growth of a true faith by broadcasting descriptions of our latest bombers or promises of clothing and food packets. For the afflicted the one and only road to faith is through the virtue of spiritual poverty. But this is a cryptic truth. For spiritual poverty appears to resemble resignation to slavery. And it is indeed almost identical with it, except for an infinitely small difference. We are always brought back to something infinitely small, which is infinitely more than everything.

Affliction is not in itself a school of spiritual poverty; but it offers almost the only opportunity of learning it. And although affliction is much less fleeting than happiness, it does pass away; so we need to make haste.

Are we going to take this opportunity? From the military point of view this question is perhaps more important than strategy, and from the economic point of view more important than statistics and distribution tables. Hitler has taught us, if we are capable of learning, that a truly realistic policy takes account first and foremost of thoughts.

He hopes for the triumph of evil; his material is the mass, the dough. We hope for the triumph of good; our material is the yeast. The difference of material calls for different methods.

To anyone who does actually consent to directing his attention and love beyond the world, towards the reality that exists outside the reach of all human faculties, it is given to succeed in doing so. In that case, sooner or later, there descends upon him a part of the good, which shines through him upon all that surrounds him.

The combination of these two facts — the longing in the depth of the heart for absolute good, and the power, though only latent, of directing attention and love to a reality beyond the world and of receiving good from it — constitutes a link which attaches every man without exception to that other reality.

Whoever recognizes that reality recognizes also that link. Because of it, he holds every human being without any exception as something sacred to which he is bound to show respect.

This is the only possible motive for universal respect towards all human beings. Whatever formulation of belief or disbelief a man may choose to make, if his heart inclines him to feel this respect, then he in fact also recognizes a reality other than this world's reality. Whoever in fact does not feel this respect is alien to that other reality also.

The reality of the world we live in is composed of variety. Unequal objects unequally solicit our attention. Certain people personally attract our attention, either through the hazard of circumstances or some chance affinity. For the lack of such circumstances or affinity other people remain unidentified. They escape our attention or, at the most, it only sees them as items of a collectivity.

If our attention is entirely confined to this world it is entirely subject to the effect of these inequalities, which it is all the less able to resist because it is unaware of it.

It is impossible to feel equal respect for things that are in fact unequal unless the respect is given to something that is identical in all of them. Men are unequal in all their relations with the things of this world, without exception. The only thing that is identical in all men is the presence of a link with the reality outside the world.

All human beings are absolutely identical insofar as they can be thought of as consisting of a center, which is an unquenchable desire for good, surrounded by an accretion of physical and bodily matter.

Only by really directing the attention beyond the world can there be real contact with this central and essential fact of human nature. Only an attention thus directed possesses the faculty, always identical in all cases, of irradiating with light any human being whatsoever.

If anyone possesses this faculty, then his attention is in reality directed beyond the world, whether he is aware of it or not.

The link which attaches the human being to the reality outside the world is, like the reality itself, beyond the reach of human faculties. The respect that it inspires as soon as it is recognized cannot be expressed to it.

This respect cannot, in this world, find any form of direct expression. But unless it is expressed it has no existence. There is a possibility of indirect expression for it.

The respect inspired by the link between man and the reality outside the world can be expressed to that part of man which exists in the reality of this world.

The reality of this world is necessity. The part of man which is in this world is the part which is in bondage to necessity and subject to the misery of need.

The one possibility of indirect expression of respect for the human being is offered by men's needs, the needs of the soul and of the body, in this world.

It is based upon the connection in human nature between the desire for good, which is the essence of man, and his sensibility. There is never any justification for doubting the existence in any man of this connection.

Because of it, when a man's life is destroyed or damaged by some wound or privation of soul or body, which is due to other men's actions or negligence, it is not only his sensibility that suffers but also his aspiration towards the good. Therefore, there has been sacrilege towards that which is sacred in him.

On the other hand, there are cases where it is only man's sensibility that is affected; for example, where his wound or privation is solely the result of the blind working of natural forces, or where he recognizes that the people who seem to be making him suffer are far from bearing him any ill will, but are acting solely in obedience to a necessity which he also acknowledges.

The possibility of indirect expression of respect for the human being is the basis of obligation. Obligation is concerned with the needs in this world of the souls and bodies of human beings, whoever they may be. For each need there is a corresponding obligation; for each obligation a corresponding need. There is no other kind of obligation, so far as human affairs are concerned.

If there seem to be others, they are either false or else it is only by error that they have not been classed among the obligations mentioned.

Anyone whose attention and love are really directed towards the reality outside the world recognizes at the same time that he is bound, both in public and private life, by the single and permanent obligation to remedy, according to his responsibilities and to the extent of his power, all the privations of soul and body which are liable to destroy or damage the earthly life of any human being whatsoever.

This obligation cannot legitimately be held to be limited by the insufficiency of power or the nature of the responsibilities until everything possible has been done to explain the necessity of the limitation to those who will suffer by it; the explanation must be completely truthful and must be such as to make it possible for them to acknowledge the necessity.

No combination of circumstances ever cancels this obligation. If there are circumstances which seem to cancel it as regards a certain man or category of men, they impose it in fact all the more imperatively.

The thought of this obligation is present to all men, but in very different forms and in very varying degrees of clarity. Some men are more and some are less inclined to accept — or to refuse — it as their rule of conduct.

Its acceptance is usually mixed with self-deception, and even when it is quite sincere it is not consistently acted upon. To refuse it is to become criminal.

The proportions of good and evil in any society depend partly upon the proportion of consent to that of refusal and partly upon the distribution of power between those who consent and those who refuse.

If any power of any kind is in the hands of a man who has not given total, sincere, and enlightened consent to this obligation such power is misplaced.

If a man has willfully refused to consent, then it is in itself a criminal activity for him to exercise any function, major or minor, public or private, which gives him control over people's lives. All those who, with knowledge of his mind, have acquiesced in his exercise of the function are accessories to the crime.

Any State whose whole official doctrine constitutes an incitement to this crime is itself wholly criminal. It can retain no trace of legitimacy.

Any State whose official doctrine is not primarily directed against this crime in all its forms is lacking in full legitimacy.

Any legal system which contains no provisions against this crime is without the essence of legality. Any legal system which provides against some forms of this crime but not others is without the full character of legality.

Any government whose members commit this crime, or authorize it in their subordinates, has betrayed its function.

Any collectivity, institution, or form of collective life whatsoever whose normal functioning implies or induces the practice of this crime is convicted *ipso facto* of illegitimacy and should be reformed or abolished.

Any man who has any degree of influence, however small, upon public opinion becomes an accessory to this crime if he refrains from denouncing it whenever it comes to his knowledge, or if he purposely avoids knowledge of it in order not to have to denounce it.

A country is not innocent of this crime if public opinion, being free to express itself, does not denounce any current example of it, or if, freedom of expression being forbidden, the crime is not denounced clandestinely.

It is the aim of public life to arrange that all forms of power are entrusted, so far as possible, to men who effectively consent to be bound by the obligation towards all human beings which lies upon everyone, and who understand the obligation.

Law is the totality of the permanent provisions for making this aim effective.

To understand the obligation involves two things: understanding the principle and understanding its application.

Since it is with human needs in this world that the application is concerned, it is for the intelligence to conceive the idea of need and to discern, discriminate, and enumerate, with all the accuracy of which it is capable, the earthly needs of the soul and of the body.

This is a study which is permanently open to revision.

Statement of Obligations

A concrete conception of obligation towards human beings and a subdivision of it into a number of obligations is obtained by conceiving the earthly needs of the body and of the human soul. Each need entails a corresponding obligation.

The needs of a human being are sacred. Their satisfaction cannot be subordinated either to reasons of state, or to any consideration of money, nationality, race, or color, or to the moral or other value attributed to the human being in question, or to any consideration whatsoever.

There is no legitimate limit to the satisfaction of the needs of a human being except as imposed by necessity and by the needs of other human beings. The limit is legitimate only if the needs of all human beings receive an equal degree of attention.

The fundamental obligation towards human beings is subdivided into a number of concrete obligations by the enumeration of the essential needs of the human being. Each need is related to an obligation, and each obligation to a need.

The needs in question are earthly needs, for those are the only ones that man can satisfy. They are needs of the soul as well as of the body; for the soul has needs whose non-satisfaction leaves it in a state analogous to that of a starved or mutilated body.

The principal needs of the human body are food, warmth,

sleep, health, rest, exercise, fresh air. The needs of the soul can for the most part be listed in pairs of opposites which balance and complete one another.

The human soul has need of equality and of hierarchy.

Equality is the public recognition, effectively expressed in institutions and manners, of the principle that an equal degree of attention is due to the needs of all human beings. Hierarchy is the scale of responsibilities. Since attention is inclined to direct itself upwards and remain fixed, special provisions are necessary to ensure the effective compatibility of equality and hierarchy.

The human soul has need of consented obedience and of liberty.

Consented obedience is what one concedes to an authority because one judges it to be legitimate. It is not possible in relation to a political power established by conquest or coup d'état nor to an economic power based upon money.

Liberty is the power of choice within the latitude left between the direct constraint of natural forces and the authority accepted as legitimate. The latitude should be sufficiently wide for liberty to be more than a fiction, but it should include only what is innocent and should never be wide enough to permit certain kinds of crime.

The human soul has need of truth and of freedom of expression.

The need for truth requires that intellectual culture should be universally accessible, and that it should be able to be acquired in an environment neither physically remote nor psychologically alien. It requires that in the domain of thought there should never be any physical or moral pressure exerted for any purpose other than an exclusive concern for truth, which implies an absolute ban on all propaganda without exception. It calls for protection against error and lies; which means that every avoidable material falsehood publicly asserted becomes a punishable offense. It calls for public health measures against poisons in the domain of thought.

But, in order to be exercised, the intelligence requires to be free to express itself without control by any authority. There must therefore be a domain of pure intellectual research, separate but accessible to all, where no authority intervenes.

The human soul has need of some solitude and privacy and also of some social life.

The human soul has need of both personal property and collective property.

Personal property never consists in the possession of a sum of money, but in the ownership of concrete objects like a house, a field, furniture, tools, which seem to the soul to be an extension of itself and of the body. Justice requires that personal property, in this sense, should be, like liberty, inalienable.

Collective property is not defined by a legal title but by the feeling among members of a human milieu that certain objects are like an extension or development of the milieu. This feeling is only possible in certain objective conditions.

The existence of a social class defined by the lack of personal and collective property is as shameful as slavery.

The human soul has need of punishment and of honor.

Whenever a human being, through the commission of a crime, has become exiled from good, he needs to be reintegrated with it through suffering. The suffering should be inflicted with the aim of bringing the soul to recognize freely some day that its infliction was just. This reintegration with the good is what punishment is. Every man who is innocent, or who has finally expiated guilt, needs to be recognized as honorable to the same extent as anyone else.

The human soul has need of disciplined participation in a common task of public value, and it has need of personal initiative within this participation.

The human soul has need of security and also of risk. The fear of violence or of hunger or of any other extreme evil is a sickness of the soul. The boredom produced by a complete absence of risk is also a sickness of the soul.

The human soul needs above all to be rooted in several natural environments and to make contact with the universe through them.

Examples of natural human environment are: a man's country, and places where his language is spoken, and places with a culture or a historical past which he shares, and his professional milieu, and his neighborhood.

Everything which has the effect of uprooting a man or of preventing him from becoming rooted is criminal.

Any place where the needs of human beings are satisfied can be recognized by the fact that there is a flowering of fraternity, joy, beauty, and happiness. Wherever people are lonely and turned in on themselves, wherever there is sadness or ugliness, there are privations that need remedying.

Practical Application

For this statement to become the practical inspiration of the country's life, the first condition is that it should be adopted by the people with that intention.

The second condition is that anyone who wields or desires to wield any power of any kind — political, administrative, legal, economic, technical, spiritual, or other — should have to pledge himself to adopt it as his practical rule of conduct.

In such cases the equal and universal character of the obligation is to some extent modified by the particular responsibilities attaching to a particular office. It would therefore be necessary to amplify the pledge with the words: "... paying special attention to the needs of the human beings who are in my charge."

The violation of such a pledge, either in word or deed, should always in principle be punishable. But, in most cases, the institutions and public morals which would make such punishment possible would take several generations to create.

Assent to this Statement implies a continual effort to bring such institutions and such morals into existence as rapidly as possible.

Epilogue

Praise to God and compassion for creatures.

It is the same movement of heart.

But how is this possible, since the two are in obvious contradiction?

To thank God because of his great glory, and to have pity for creatures because of their wretchedness.

To have pity for Christ who was thirsty and hungry and tired.

Thankfulness to God and compassion for every creature.

Praise to God and pity for every creature.

A creature cannot legitimately be the object of any love except compassion.

Nor can God be the object of any love other than praise. . . .

Compassion for every creature, because it is far from the Good. Infinitely far. Abandoned.

God abandons our whole entire being — flesh, blood, sensibility, intelligence, love — to the pitiless necessity of matter and the cruelty of the devil, except for the eternal and supernatural part of the soul.

The creation is an abandonment. In creating what is other than Himself, God necessarily abandoned it. He only keeps under his care the part of creation which is Himself — the uncreated part of every creature. That is the life, the Light, the Word; it is the presence here below of God's only Son.

It is sufficient if we consent to this ordering of things.

How can this consent be united with compassion? How is it an act of unique love, when it seems irreconcilable with love?

Wisdom, teach me this.

God is absent from the world, except in the existence in this world of those in whom His love is alive. Therefore they ought to be present in the world through compassion. Their compassion is the visible presence of God here below.

When we are lacking in compassion we make a violent separation between a creature and God.

Through compassion we can put the created, temporal part of a creature in communication with God.

It is a marvel analogous to the act of creation itself.

The cruelty of the Jews and the Romans had so much power over Christ that it caused him to feel abandoned by God.

Compassion is what spans this abyss which creation has opened between God and the creature.

It is the rainbow.

Compassion should have the same dimension as the act of creation. It cannot exclude a single creature.

One should love oneself only with a compassionate love.

Every created thing is an object for compassion because it is ephemeral.

Every created thing is an object for compassion because it is limited.

Compassion directed towards oneself is humility.

Humility is the only permitted form of self-love.

Praise for God, compassion for creatures, humility for oneself.

Without humility, all the virtues are finite. Only humility makes them infinite. (FLN 102–3)